People of the Good God

MONGREL EMPIRE PRESS
NORMAN, OKLAHOMA, UNITED STATES OF AMERICA

2015

FIRST EDITION, 2014

People of the Good God
© 2015 by Hardy Jones

ISBN 978-0-9903204-2-5

Except for fair use in reviews and/or scholarly considerations, no part of this book may be reproduced, performed, recorded, or otherwise transmitted without the written consent of the author and the permission of the publisher.

Cover Image
"Arrival of the Acadians" © 1995 by Robert Dafford

MONGREL EMPIRE PRESS
NORMAN, OK

ONLINE CATALOGUE: WWW.MONGRELEMPIRE.ORG

This publisher is a proud member of

COUNCIL OF LITERARY MAGAZINES & PRESSES
www.clmp.org

Book Design: Mongrel Empire Press using iWork Pages

Table of Contents

A Cajun in the Heartland	1
Mudbug Come Clean	5
Gumbo, Boudin, Coubillion	13
I Got Me a Baby Bull!	19
Blessings from a Woman of the Good God	29
Rendez-vous des Cadiens Prairie	37
The Wealthiest Accordion Player	61
Lunch avec Monsieur Doucet	67
Cajun Dreams	73
Dry Gumbo	79

Acknowledgments

I must thank all the Acadians, Cajuns, and Creoles who endured to create the culture I am part of. I would like to thank Randall Kenan for his initial guidance with this project. I thank Rilla Askew, Darrell Bourque, and Larry D. Thomas for taking time to read a draft of the manuscript. Several journal editors helped bring chapters to the reading public, and I would like to thank Shane Rasmussen of *Louisiana Folklife*, Lynn Morgan Spreen of *Straitjackets*, M.L. Weber of *Sugar Mule*, and Amy Susan Wilson of *Red Truck Review*. I appreciate Jeanetta Calhoun Mish and Mongrel Empire Press for bringing this book to the world. I am thankful for the financial support provided by a research grant from the Louisiana Division of the Arts in 2001. Lastly, I thank my wife Natthinee Khot-asa Jones for her love and support.

The following works, in slightly different forms, appeared in the following journals:

"Dry Gumbo" in *Red Truck Review*; nominated by *Red Truck Review* for a 2015 Pushcart Prize.

"*Rendez-vous des Cadiens* Prairie," "Cajun Dreams" (published as "Grab Yourself a Cup of Coffee"), "Blessings from a Woman of the Good God" in *Louisiana Folklife*.

"Lunch *avec Monsieur* Doucet," "The Wealthiest Accordion Player," "Cajun Realization" in *Straitjackets*.

"I Got Me a Baby Bull" in *Sugar Mule*.

"Mudbug Come Clean" in *Miranda Literary Review*.

People
of the
Good God

Hardy Jones

"Cajuns are a people? I thought it was just a food."

—College Freshman circa 2010

A Cajun in the Heartland

In an Iowa City bar I realized I was Cajun. It was the summer of 1998, I had just graduated from LSU with my English BA, and before starting the MFA at the University of Memphis in the fall, I attended the University of Iowa's Summer Writing Festival. After the opening night's workshop, some of my fellow scribblers and I went for drinks. We'd all introduced ourselves a few hours earlier in class, and I had stated that I was from south Louisiana. This admission signaled that I was getting closer to claiming my Cajun ancestry; until then I had always made a point of stressing that I was from Florida, proudly proclaiming my hometown Pensacola.

A pint of Guinness sat in front of me and the six of us crammed around a table while an acoustic bluesman moaned on the stage.

"Hardy," a psychologist from Denver asked, "being from Louisiana, are you Cajun?"

I took a drink, thought about Uncle Dub's accordion playing, Mom's delicious gumbos, and for the first time I said: "Yes. I am."

Eurydice, a second-generation Greek from Chicago, said, "You're the first Cajun I've ever met."

Agreeing nods followed from the rest.

Instantly I felt other from these fellow Americans, who physically did not look any differently than I. Cajuns, after all, do not have a homogeneous physical type. We are set apart by culture, and being raised away from our homeland for the first fourteen years of my life, clues to my ethnic identity were not readily available. Mom, yes, was Cajun: born and raised in the southwest Louisiana marshy, pine woods. A boy from Pensacola with the most Anglo of surnames was not.

Mom was born a Felice and despite being family, these folk were mysterious. I understood that they were not run-of-the-mill poor white rural Southerners, for that group made Cajuns the butt of jokes. In popular society, little is known about us except stereotypes, and using them as guidelines it would be assumed I am a slow-witted, rowdy, two-fisted drinker who eats anything that moves. Quite an image, and one I never saw myself fitting nor wanting to. Maybe, deep inside, that was why I missed all of the obvious hints to my Cajun identity: Embarrassment, shame, not wanting to be classified as inferior.

If I had been hesitant to acknowledge that I was Cajun for fear that others would think less of me, that fear was confirmed by my workshop-mates' faces. In my youth, their looks would have unsettled me; instead, they ignited a two year search for my Cajun identity.

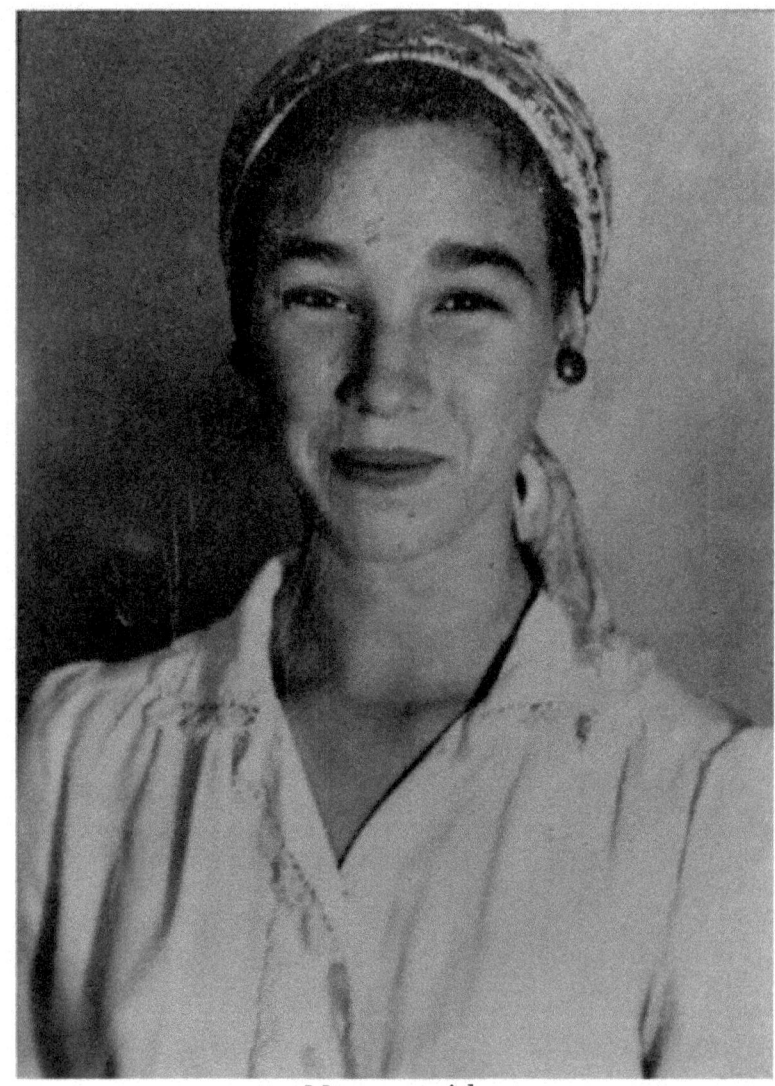

Mom as a girl.

Mudbug Come Clean

On December 20th, 1972, I was born to a Texas Dad and a Cajun Mom. Dad was the only son of a nouveau riche Texas family, and Grandfather Jones made his small fortune with timber and sawmills around East Texas and Southwest Louisiana. While families waited in Depression-era soup lines, Dad attended Alan Military Academy and received a weekly allowance of a dollar. Mom was the middle child of a dozen siblings in a poor Cajun family. *Grandpère* Felice actually worked for Grandfather Jones during the Depression, cutting timber for the latter's paper-mill in Lake Charles, Louisiana. Back then my parents did not know each other; however, according to Mom they had one brief encounter when Grandfather Jones, driven by Dad, delivered *Grandpère* Felice's paycheck.

Mom was a young girl, and when they arrived, she sat in a chinaberry tree. "You better get down from there, little girl," Grandfather Jones said, "or you're gonna hurt yourself."

Mom swung down monkey-like, landing in front of Grandfather Jones; he passed away in the 1950s, two decades before Mom and Dad married, so this was the lone time she met her future father-in-law.

"Is Kenney Felice home?"

"Yes, sir," Mom answered. Her eyes wandered past the stocky, bossy man to the car and the young driver, whose hair was cropped close, military-style. Dad smiled, knowing nothing of their second meeting to come thirty odd years later in a Lake Charles restaurant. At their second meeting Dad would be a cross-country truck driver in his late fifties with a gray receding hairline that formed an eagle's profile on top of his head. And he would be fresh from his sixth wife, having finalized the divorce the day before he met Mom.

While Dad married six times between his first and second meeting with Mom, she only married once. At the ripe age of fifteen and a half, she married a rice sharecropper named Clovis Richard. She and Clovis had seven children together—three boys and four girls, in that order—while they lived on the Illinois Plantation in Hayes, Louisiana. According to Mom, during their marriage Clovis became an alcoholic and developed a Valium habit after his right leg was crushed in a farming accident. Mom stayed in the marriage for twenty years, until his addictions and violence became intolerable. The last night Mom spent with Clovis, he chased her out of the house with a pistol. They lived on a peninsula in the marsh and the only way to get to the mainland was on the ferry that ran during the day. With nowhere to run, Mom hid behind some oak trees and watched Clovis, drunk and staggering, cursing her in French from the front porch before going into the house and passing out. At sunrise, Mom, covered with mosquito bites, slipped in the house and packed a suitcase, hid it in the washroom, and then cooked breakfast for the children and Clovis. This was during the spring, so he left early that morning to check the levees in the fields. After she got the children off to school, Mom drove to Lake Charles, got a room in a boarding house and a job as a waitress.

A few weeks later at the restaurant she met Dad.

He took a seat in the second booth from the door, and when Mom brought him a glass of water and a menu, he said, "Sit down."

"I'm working. And I don't know you."

"Well, that's how you get to know people, by talking with them."

"What do you want to eat?"

"A thick steak, cooked rare with a little blood in the middle, a baked potato, a salad, and a beer. Michelob Draft." Mom wrote the order and refused to make eye contact, but Dad never took his off her.

Dad's stubbornness kept him from giving up on his pursuit of Mom. He called for more beers, extra napkins, ketchup—which he didn't even eat—all to keep her within earshot. When Mom brought the ketchup, Dad asked her what time her shift ended.

"Why do you want to know?"

"So I'll know what time to take you dancing."

"I can't go dancing. I've got to open in the morning."

Dad came up with a compromise. They would go dancing at the Carousel Bar, only a block away, and he'd have her back at the boarding house at a decent hour. True to his word, Dad only kept her out a couple of hours, and when he walked her to the boarding house's front door, he said, "I'll be calling you."

Mom didn't believe him.

Dad drove for a moving company and had to make a haul, but four days later, to Mom's surprise, she received a call at the restaurant.

"Put your dancing shoes on," Dad said, "I'm coming to town."

After a few more dances and a couple of drinks at the Carousel, she explained her situation, figuring that would make him lose interest in her. "I'm afraid to try and get a divorce," she said. "Clovis can get me for desertion. Then I won't even be able to see my kids."

"Don't worry," Dad said, stroking her hand. "We'll get your kids, and get you a divorce. I've got an attorney friend in Pensacola who'll take care of everything."

That is Mom's version of the story, which I have pieced together over the last four decades. Dad, who died when I was 18, always claimed that he was unaware of Mom's other children until she returned from Louisiana with my four older half-sisters. I was around four months old at that time and we lived in Pensacola, when Mom's daughters, labeled by Dad as "the girls," came to live with us. My first memory of "the girls" was Dad telling me: "They're not your real sisters. You're my son. A Jones. Their daddy is a coonass who shot himself."

What should have been a joyous occasion, the melding of two families, was anything but. Dad felt lied to and burdened with another man's children; and his insistence that I was a Jones, separate from my half-siblings, was the first roadblock to my understanding that I was Cajun.

When they began dating, did Mom recognize Dad's surname as that of her father's boss? If the meeting at her parents' home did indeed occur, did Mom recall the day in the chinaberry tree when she dated Dad? Or was that story Mom refashioning her history?

I love the story of my parents' first meeting, but I'm not sure it transpired. Dad never spoke of it, but perhaps he did not due his anger at feeling tricked into raising "the girls." Mom is the only one alive from that supposed meeting, and the more I think about the story, piece together ages and timelines, I feel I must categorize the story as romantic mythology.

***

Although I was born in Florida, I was conceived, so my parents told me, at a motel in Franklin, Louisiana. In reference to my conception, Dad said: "Your mama took everything serious that I poked at her in fun." They attended the Crawfish Festival during the day, and those red mudbugs, which resemble mini-lobsters with a sweet tasting tail and a head full of spicy juice, are allegedly an aphrodisiac. Considering that Dad was fifty-five and Mom was thirty-seven, crawfish could have played a role in my conception.

Every few summers we drove from Pensacola to southwest Louisiana, north of Lake Charles, and visited Mom's parents, who lived on a dirt road, Felice Cut-off, named after my *Grand-grandpère* Homer Felice. The area was extremely rural, dominated by pine forests, marshes, and rice fields. Relatives, close and distant, abounded, and since they filled the woods around Felice Cut-off, the area was unofficially called *Feliceville*. *Grandpère* Felice was in his 70's the first time I met him, and I never saw his lanky body in anything except denim overalls. He stood close to six feet two and at his heaviest weighed 162 pounds.

Grandmère Felice was a short stout woman who bore twelve children; nine lived to adulthood. Her last three children—her second pair of fraternal twins and a boy—were stillborn. *Grandmère* Felice possessed thick upper arms and forearms that bespoke of a hard life raising many children and running a farm. *Grandpère* and *Grandmère* Felice had false teeth that neither saw much reason to wear, and they both dipped snuff, so I couldn't sit in a chair that didn't have an old coffee can stuffed with paper towels. No one I knew in Florida dipped snuff, so this was an activity that, in my youth, I associated only with Cajuns.

Grandpère used Garret Powder snuff that came in a tin can wrapped in red paper, with yellow trim and a coat of arms on the back. One day I asked him for a dip. He had me stand in front of him and bend my knees so he could see into my mouth as he filled the left side of it with nicotine sand. I pulled away before he finished pouring and some fell on the floor. I hurried to the sink and washed that foul powder out of my mouth. *Grandpère* didn't say anything, but I could tell he was disappointed. Practically all the other grandchildren were raised in *Feliceville*, saw *Grandpère* daily, and all the boys dipped snuff. But not me: I was the strange grandson from Florida.

During these summer visits, Mom's siblings, especially Aunt Emma Dale, in her nasal-whine, always asked when she was moving back.

"Ain't you tired of Florida yet?" Aunt Emma Dale said through her bulging dip of snuff.

"Louisiana's got too many swamps in it," I said. "I don't want to live here."

"Florida's got swamps too," Aunt Emma Dale said.

"But you ain't gotta live in them like here," I said.

Mom cut me some eyes that told me I was out of bounds.

But I didn't want to be around these uneducated, tobacco-chewing, rural people with whom I felt no kinship. When I was fourteen, however, against my pleading we moved to Louisiana; but it was Dad, not Mom, who initiated our move. The reason he wanted out of Pensacola: it was becoming too big with too many temptations for his namesake. I think, however, that Dad had another reason: he had a heart attack four years earlier from which he momentarily died. We had no family in Florida and Dad did not have contact with the remaining Joneses in Texas, so I believe our move to Louisiana was his way of providing a support system for me and Mom.

Our first house in Louisiana was a few miles south of *Feliceville* and sat next to a rice field and its pump-house, inside which the pump whirred night and day, flooding the fields. The first thing I noticed about our new place wasn't the ranch-style house or the fact that we were in the country, a half-hour from town; it was mini-mud towers, soft gray in color, that stood a few inches above the ground and dotted our yard. These were crawfish holes, where the animals came out of the ground. If the rice field and its noisy pump wasn't enough to remind me that I was no longer in Florida, having crawfish in my yard did.

In 1986, we lived there for three months, long enough for me to finish eighth grade at South Beauregard School, which housed, in multiple buildings, kindergarten through twelfth grade. Once there, I discovered beaucoup cousins, most of whom were either in elementary school or high school—I was born in a gap in which there were no relatives my age—making it awkward for us to have much in common. Coming from an urban Catholic school, this public rural one was culture shock: students in cowboy boots and teachers with Cajun accents.

At South Beauregard School, my social studies class from Florida was replaced by Louisiana History. I don't remember if the Acadian refugees who evolved into present-day Cajuns were mentioned in class, but it wouldn't have mattered; in my youth I didn't embrace my roots. I loved having a Mom who could out-cook anyone in the neighborhood back in Pensacola, but all the same I was proud to be from Florida. I see now that it was a pride of vanity, one built around an idyllic image of beach-living and convenient malls with loud, lighted arcades, which as a child were what I wanted to be a part of. I wanted no part of Louisiana and Cajuns on dirt roads dipping snuff.

For all of my youthful complaining, today I am happy we moved to Louisiana. My presence there enabled me to experience our homeland. If we had remained in Florida, my understanding of south Louisiana would have been limited to those short summer visits. While a teenager, I thought: what could these folk who spoke funny English teach me? Now, I understand that they taught me a pivotal lesson: where half of me originated.

Mom and Dad in the mid-1970s.

Gumbo, Boudin, Coubillion

Cajun food is our culture's pride and joy. It's no wonder then that gumbo was the earliest clue that should have slapped me in the face and said: Hardy, you are Cajun.

It didn't slap back then, but I felt the sting twenty-five years later, remembering how in third grade Jonathan Garret told me his family had gone out for gumbo. Jonathan's family paying money for a dish that during the winter was a staple in my house confused me; as far as I knew, part of a mom's job description was cooking gumbo, and thus I assumed Jonathan's mom was not a good cook.

Later, our neighbors from across the street invited me over for some of their gumbo. A retired couple, Fay and W.D. were both from Alabama, and Fay was a short woman with a wrinkled face that resembled a roadmap, which was ironic because when I knew her, she was in her sixties and still didn't know how to drive. Her lack of skill, I soon discovered, was not limited to driving.

At that point in my life, I had only eaten Mom's gumbo, usually seafood full of shrimp and blue-crabs, or chicken and sausage. I was not ready for what Fay cooked. To begin with, she did not put any *filé*—powdered sassafras leaves—in it, and this is what gives gumbo its distinctive consistency and taste. Adding insult to injury, Fay cooked her rice in with the gumbo

—major faux pas. Rice is to be cooked separately and the gumbo spooned on top of it.

Although Fay's gumbo lacked *filé* it had its share of ingredients: shrimp, oysters, and chicken. The shrimp and oysters I was accustomed to, but not the chicken with them. Mom cooked seafood gumbo or chicken gumbo, not this amalgamation. Fay's gumbo also had corn, peas, and carrots: ingredients I never had before and hope never again to experience in a gumbo.

Fay's house that night was full of her family. Her kitchen and dining area was one large room with a rectangular table flanked by wooden benches in the center of it; the table was packed with adults, while her grandchildren and I sat on the floor around the coffee table.

In the middle of the boisterous dining, Fay sought my opinion of the meal. Being only a decade old, I knew nothing of the etiquette a guest was to display, so over the familial cacophony, I announced, "This ain't gumbo."

Thankfully, Fay overlooked my rude truthfulness and the others resumed conversing and eating. I didn't finish my bowl of "gumbo," soon walked home, and upon entering, Mom asked: "How was it?"

"Not as good as yours," I said and gave her a run-down of the ingredients.

"She made a chowder."

Fay's gumbo was brought up around the house only a few times after that, and always pejoratively.

***

While Mom was reluctant to teach me her mother tongue, food helped me learn my first Cajun words. Boudin, rice dressing—otherwise known as dirty rice—stuffed into sausage casing, was something Dad made sure to pick up a few pounds of when we visited Mom's family. Boudin is one of those words I've always known, hearing it said around the house by both parents, and Dad pronounced it just as smoothly as Mom: boo-dah[n]. I rarely pronounce the "n" and didn't even know the word had one until I was twelve.

Boudin is boiled in grocery store meat markets, small sausage kitchens, and service stations all over south Louisiana. The summer of my twelfth year we bought a Styrofoam ice chest from the store where we bought the boudin; on the side of the cooler, in bright red letters, was the store's name: the Boudin Kitchen.

"What's boudin?" I asked from the backseat, pronouncing the "n" on the end for the first time.

"What, son?" Mom said.

"Boudin?" I repeated, not as loudly, for the connection was starting to come together in my mind.

"Boudin," Mom said, pronouncing it in Cajun, the sound swooshing softly from her mouth. She turned and looked at me incredulously.

I didn't follow up that outburst with any more stupid questions. But in retrospect, it wasn't too dumb for a child raised in a virtually all English world. And French words, in comparison to run-of-the-mill American English, sound grandiose and eloquent. Until a few years ago, I didn't realize that the tasty catfish *coubillion* with its tender white fillets and spicy tomato gravy, meant simply catfish soup. Mom's chicken *fricassée*, boiled chicken in a dark-brown gravy served over white rice, was to die for. The meat slid effortlessly off the bone and the peppery gravy made the rice worth eating all by itself, which I often did after the chicken was gone. I was dismayed to learn that *fricassée* means stew.

Food was my earliest and biggest indicator that I was Cajun, and I missed it. I am somewhat embarrassed to admit how blind I was to this fact, but growing up with these foods made them a natural part of my life, even in the Florida panhandle. And when something is so natural, one has a tendency to take it for granted. If I had paid attention in my youth and noticed that Mom was the only one in the neighborhood cooking gumbo, *coubillion*, and *fricassée*, it may not have taken me a quarter of a century to understand that I, like Mom, am Cajun.

In order to retain authenticity, these recipes are written as Mom told them to me.

Mom's Seafood Gumbo

First make a roux in an iron skillet (45 minutes of constant stirring).

Add water to roux.

Clean shrimp (according to Mom, small shrimp are more flavorful), crabs, and oysters in a sink and set aside.

Fill a large pot with water and when it reaches a boil put in the seafood. Green onions, 2 cloves of garlic, salt and pepper, and 1 teaspoon of cayenne (these are approximations by Mom; she cooks by feel)

Cook for 1-3 hours. Slow cooking is preferred in order to intensify the flavor of the seafood. Stir slowly so as not to break up the seafood. Stir often so the gumbo does not stick to the bottom of the pot. Add *filé* when you turn off the fire and stir it in.

For the best flavor, allow the gumbo to set and eat it the following day. If you cannot wait, then by all means dig in immediately.

Mom's Chicken and Sausage Gumbo

Make a roux in an iron skillet (45 minutes of constant stirring). When prepared, the roux should be golden brown. Add water to roux.

Heat a half pot of water and pour roux into water.

Wash and cut up a whole fryer and cut up your Cajun sausage. Put in your chicken and sausage. Cook over a low fire for 1-3 hours. Stir often and slowly. Make a pot of rice. Serve over rice.

Mom's Coubillion

2 teaspoons butter, ½ cup finely chopped onion, ½ cup parsley leaves, large can of tomato sauce. 2 lbs.

Catfish fillets (add more for larger crowds. This recipe is for 4 diners).

Cook over low heat for 2-3 hours, stirring often so it won't stick to the pot.

Mom's Chicken Fricassée

Make a roux from flour until golden brown.

Place the roux in a large pot and add water.

Place chicken in slowly a piece at a time and then let the chicken cook in the roux for 30-45 minutes, depending on the size of the chicken pieces. (slice thighs in half to cook quicker).

1 white onion, chopped, and add it as you add the chicken.

Cook a pot of rice.

Season the chicken to taste using salt, black pepper, cayenne, and garlic. Eat over rice.

I Got Me a Baby Bull!

"I'm putting off that surgery as long as I can," Mom said.

We drove north on Highway 171, a small two-lane state highway, home to DeRidder. It was a little after four in the afternoon, and the sun hung low and golden to our left. I had taken Mom, Janell Ernst, to her doctor in Lake Charles and he found adhesions in her stomach. To end the pain she experienced after eating, he told her surgery was necessary: a laser would burn the adhesions.

Mom didn't want any more operations; she'd had five in the last eight years. These included three arthroscopic knee operations—scopes, she called them—two on the left, one on the right, and the installation of an artificial right knee. After a nickel-sized tumor was discovered during a mammogram, her most recent surgery was a modified radical mastectomy on her right breast.

"I'll stick to drinking Slim-Fast. My stomach doesn't hurt as much then."

"With the laser, the surgery shouldn't hurt that bad," I said.

"That's what they said about those scopes. But those jokers hurt." She crossed her hands on her lap and pulled her mouth tight. Mom was a rotund woman standing 5' 3"; her well-defined cheekbones and almond-shaped eyes, which shut when she laughed, exhibited the Native American lineage inherited from her grandmother.

I didn't know what to tell her about the surgery.

"We're still stopping at Estelle's?" I asked.

"We'll have to make it short. I want to get home so you can feed the cows before it gets dark."

Estelle Richard, no relation to Mom's first husband, was an old friend of Mom's, really more like an auntie.

That morning I'd said: "Estelle can tell me how to trill my 'R's in Cajun."

"I told you," Mom said, "just put your tongue at the top of your mouth and pull it down quick."

I'd tried that, but it didn't work consistently. "Estelle might have a short-cut for me."

"She doesn't have much education," Mom said. "And she was brought up talking Cajun. She's not going to be able to explain how to speak it."

I knew, most likely, this was true. When I was in elementary school, I tried to get Mom to teach me Cajun, but she always said: "The French I know is a slang. You don't want to learn that." Despite not receiving formal lessons from Mom, I picked up simple greetings: hello, good-bye, how are you? I figured it wasn't that Mom didn't want to teach me Cajun, but that she simply couldn't. She stopped regularly attending school in sixth grade and quit in eighth grade to marry. While illiterate in Cajun and possessing basic ability in English, Mom was the one who worked with me in elementary school on my vocabulary for spelling tests and instilled the love of reading in me—quite ironic given her level of literacy.

We rounded a bend in the highway and crossed into Beauregard Parish. On our right, golden rows in the dry rice fields arced into the horizon. Next to the rice fields sat three trailer-homes spaced roughly fifty yards apart, and across the highway sat Estelle's small stained wood house; her yard and pasture were yellow and the grass looked hard. I turned in and parked just outside her carport, a simple wooden addition to the house, also unpainted.

A gust of bitter wind hit us as we walked to the house. Estelle was 87 and lived alone; her daughter Jean lived next door with her husband. Their homes were separated by a hundred yards of pasture.

Estelle's blue LTD sat in the carport. It didn't have a license plate. The tires were flat.

As Mom took the three wooden steps to the front door, she held on to the screen door's handle and I balanced her with the other hand. She knocked. No answer. She knocked again. We waited a moment. "She must be up at Jean's," Mom said. I held her hand and she walked down the steps one at a time; another blast of cold air took my breath when we walked from under the carport.

"You want to go to Jean's?"

"Let's just go on home," Mom said.

I was disappointed. Not just because I missed a chance of learning how to trill a Cajun 'R,' but I didn't want to be in the car with Mom. She was looking for an answer I didn't have. Of course I didn't want her to face another operation. There are always risks, no matter how routine the procedure. But if an operation would take away her pain, could I be against it?

The screen door squeaked behind us. We turned around.

"Hello, Estelle."

She stood behind the screen door, her mouth agape.

"It's Nell."

A knowing smile came across Estelle's wrinkled face. "Pass yourself through the door and sit down." Estelle's skin was a golden yellow. It was now dulled by her mostly gray hair, but in her younger days, her hair had been coal black and her skin shone. She and Mom were about the same height.

Estelle, in a black polyester house dress and gray slippers, sat in a green naugahyde recliner on the right side of the living room. A closed-up wood stove was to her left with an aluminum pie tin covering the stove-pipe hole. Estelle had cooked with this stove until the 1980s, when her husband Dennis bought her a gas stove from Montgomery Ward.

Mom and I sat in recliners on the left side of the living room. Color photos of babies and black and white ones of older folks hung on the walls. Two paintings hung side-by-side over a small, cluttered desk. One painting was Jesus in a white robe on His knees praying, and the other was the Virgin Mary ascending into Heaven. A black rosary encompassed both paintings.

"How you been, Estelle?" Mom asked.

"Went to the doctor. He checked my heart and said it okay. I'm not going to die today." She smiled with a closed mouth. "And I had to get 'shoes' for my walker." Shoes were Estelle's term for the rubber cushions on the bottom of her walker. "Got to use it when I check my cows. Me and Jean just got home a few hours before. She drove me to Lake Charles." Estelle waved her hands demonstratively as she spoke. When her cadence increased, so did the tempo of her hands, saying as much as her Cajun-accented English.

"We just came from the doctor too." Mom sighed. "I have to have surgery on my stomach."

"That bad, Nell." Estelle made the sign of the cross. "I don't need surgery, no. The doctor checked my heart. It miss a beat every now and then." She patted her hand on her chest. "But it still good, yeah."

Silence; the air was heavy as Estelle and Mom considered their mortality.

"What happened to your license plate?" Mom asked.

"Jean don't want me to drive. Say my actions not so fast no more."

"With my artificial knee, it's hard for me to drive," Mom said. "I can't tell how hard I'm pushing the pedal. Hardy's my chauffeur when he's home from college."

"That's good." Estelle smiled at me. "Jean don't want to drive me till it good for her. I tell her I got to go when I got to go. She took the plate off the car and the battery out, too."

Estelle grinned shyly.

"I got me a baby bull!" Estelle shook her finger, motioning to the back of the house and the barn. "When we got back, I pass to the bathtub to give my cows water. One of my heifer there licking a new calf. I call Jean and she come saw it. He pretty, black and white."

"That's good, yeah," Mom said. Ten minutes into our visit and her Cajun accent and syntax returned. "How was your Christmas, Estelle?"

"Good. I went to Jean's. My grandchildren and great-grandchildren all there."

"Only Hardy came in," Mom said.

Here is why I believe Mom's other seven children did not visit her for the holidays. She claims she ran away from Clovis because of his abuse, but in doing so, she left the children. The three eldest are boys—Wilfred, Preston, and Raymond—and they had reached the age of majority and were living on their own, but the four girls—Catherine, Rebecca, Margaret, and Barbara—were still at home, ranging from teens to an adolescent. On the day that Mom fled, they returned from school to a house with no mother. I have only heard Mom's side of the story, but returning to find their mother missing must have been traumatic. What were their initial thoughts? Did they know of the domestic abuse and think she had been the victim of foul play? Or did Clovis conceal the abuse from them? I have asked Mom if the girls knew she was being abused and she adamantly says that Catherine and Rebecca were old enough to know what was going on. I have not seen Catherine or Rebecca in roughly two decades, so I have never had the opportunity to ask them how they viewed their parents' relationship. Whether the girls knew about the abuse or not, the one certainty is that they returned to a home devoid of a mother and when they next saw their mother, she arrived unannounced at their house with a new child (me) and another man's last name.

I do not know why the girls went with Mom; I suppose her parental authority presided over them. Clovis was in the rice fields that day and when he returned, he found a vacant home. After checking with neighbors, he figured out that Mom had taken the girls, but Clovis did nothing to get the girls back. His lack of action was an admission of guilt? Did he think that his abuse had driven away his wife? And if he filed to get his daughters back, did he fear having his abuse of Mom come to light?

Which leads to another question: Why did Mom return for the girls? To be a mother to them or to hurt Clovis?

The girls and I only lived under the same roof for a few years—by the time I was in third grade, they had moved out—and I have tried to envision the day they returned home to find Mom missing. They lived in a small clapboard shack on a peninsula in the swamp, forced to take a ferry to their house. I imagine Catherine, the eldest, was the first to deduce that their mom was gone. How long did it take her? Did she first walk through the house calling, "Mama? Mama? Where are you?" Did Catherine then walk to the garden behind the house, and not seeing their mom, did she run back to the house and announce, "Mama is gone!"

Barbara was the youngest and always carried a doll with her, even to school. Was she lost in brushing her doll's hair, oblivious to the fact that her mom had not greeted her with an after school snack? Or did her age, her dependence on her mom, make her acknowledge the disappearance quicker than the older ones?

Did the girls think their mom had left for a short time, to cool off after an explosive encounter with their dad? What was the waiting like? Did they expect her to return in days, weeks, or could they fathom the possibility that their mom may be gone forever? When Mom returned with me why did they leave with her?

Whatever the girls' reason for accompanying her, returning to a motherless house is the reason they did not celebrate Christmas with Mom.

***

Jean walked up from her house wearing a purple knee length jacket and a tan mesh-scarf over her head. She was a tall, rangy woman. Her hair was onyx and her skin a creamy gold. Mom stood and they hugged in the center of the living room. Mom and Jean attended the one room school house in Ragley back in the 40's.

"How was your Christmas, Jean?" Mom asked.

"Good. The kids all came home. That was the first time all of them made it in four years. Usually one of them's got to work, or goes to the in-laws. Rest of the time I'm watching her." She pointed to Estelle. "She gets into trouble."

"I don't, no."

"The doctor don't want Mama tending her cows," Jean said. "He's afraid she'll hurt herself out there. And I am too. He asked her today if she been tending her cows."

"My cows need water. You gonna pass water to them?"

"I've done it before."

"What'd you tell the doctor?" Mom asked.

Estelle's hands stopped. She rested them on her lap and grinned. "I told him . . . ."

"She told him she don't tend her cows," Jean said, "but I do."

"You checked my bull calf," Estelle said.

"After you called me, Mama."

"But you still checked it." Estelle shook her hands, palms out, at her daughter. "Jean don't think I can drive, no. But I can, yeah. I can pass myself to the doctor. Sometimes I get lost . . ."

"Don't feel bad," Mom said, "I do too. Those cancer pills I take, they mess up my memory." The pills are actually chemotherapy in pill form, and therefore are anti-cancer. But Mom never refers to them as such.

"I took the license plate off the car because Mama ain't supposed to be driving," Jean said. "But Mama drove the car without the license plate."

Estelle smiled proudly like an obedient child who had done her one mischievous deed.

The phone rang twice. Estelle nodded at us and got up and answered it. "Hello?" After the greeting, the rest of the phone conversation was in Cajun until good-bye. I recognized the words *aujourd'hui*—today—and *docteur*, so I knew she was saying she went to the doctor today. In today's Louisiana, when most younger Cajuns like myself are not fluent, I was glad to hear a native speaker.

Estelle hung up the phone, rejoined us in the living room, and told us that was her sister checking on her.

"Hardy wants know how to roll the 'R' in Cajun," Mom said.

"I can say it on words like *trés bien*," I said. "It's when the 'R' is the first letter of a word that I have trouble."

Estelle looked to Jean; Jean looked to her mama, and then to me. I waited for the short-cut.

"Say Raymond," Jean said. She rolled the 'R.' "You feel how your tongue hit the back of your teeth?"

I nodded, yes.

"Get by yourself so folks won't make fun of you, and say that over and over."

I looked to Estelle to see what tips she had, but she only nodded in agreement with Jean.

There was no Cajun short-cut.

When I started kindergarten, I was given speech lessons because I had trouble saying words that began with "th" and "tr," so that "three" and "tree" came out as "free." As a child, I assumed that the teacher heard me speak and what she diagnosed as a speech problem—the term tongue-tied was bandied about the first decade of my life—was most likely a Cajun accent that I picked up from Mom. As an adult I asked Mom how the speech lessons came about.

"I had you placed in those classes. I knew the other kids would make fun of you and later you'd have trouble finding a good job."

Not only had Mom refused to teach me Cajun, but she eliminated the remnants of the accent. Without those classes, would it be easy for me to trill the "r?"

***

"You remember how we'd get whippings at school," Mom said, "if we got caught speaking French?"

"I got plenty of them," Jean said.

"Me too," Mom said. "I remember when I brought the note home saying that there would be no more French spoke in school. I read it to Mama, and she said 'Why can't y'all speak French? We speak it at home.' She didn't understand why, and I didn't either." Mom's voice trailed off and she took a moment before continuing: "Dub," Mom's tongue-tied twin brother, "he pledged allegiance to the flag in French to spite them. Mrs. Thorton, that old maid, she was so ugly, sent him to the principal's office. Old Principal Showers asked Dub, 'Why'd you say the pledge in French? You knew you were going to get into trouble.' And Dub said, 'It ain't my fault y'all can't understand.'" All three women laughed loud and long.

I've heard this story before; I like it, and all the other stories Mom tells me about Uncle Dub, whose given name was Wesley (He passed away before I was born. Since I never met him, I paid homage to him by appropriating his name for the protagonist of my novel *Every Bitter Thing*). Uncle Dub taught himself to play the accordion, guitar, steel guitar, and drums.

In the 1950s and 1960s he had a Cajun band that played in bars and dancehalls around Lake Charles. After that band broke up, Uncle Dub moved to Wisconsin, where his older sister my aunt Joyce lived, and got a job delivering heating oil to homes. He also started a new band: Wesley and the Jamboree Boys, with whom he made five albums. The record company forced him to primarily play country music, which meant he sang in his second language. When he spoke English Uncle Dub had a slight stutter and sounded tongue-tied, but like Mel Tillis, when he sang, his speech impediment vanished. When Mom played Uncle Dub's records, his voice was a rich baritone reminiscent of Johnny Cash.

According to Mom, Uncle Dub died the week before he was scheduled to play the Grand Old Opry. In 1965 a drunk driver hit him head-on at an intersection. Dub was in a new white Cadillac convertible and the steering wheel went through his chest.

While Uncle Dub did not become a legendary Cajun musician, I am proud that for his short time on earth he contributed to our culture's music. Since he ended up recording country music, some may think that he "sold out," but one must remember that country music had an effect on the sound of modern Cajun music. One sign of this influence is the prominent role of the steel guitar in some bands, and therefore country music is simply another ingredient in our musical gumbo.

I wish I had known Uncle Dub. Since he was Mom's twin, I know we would have been close.

***

"We better go, if we're going to get back before dark." Mom looked at me. "You still got to feed the cows." I stood and helped Mom up.

"Don't got to go so soon." Estelle walked behind us to the door.

"You had you a calf today and I got a Jersey that's pregnant," Mom said. "Now I got to go see if mine had one. It was good seeing you, Jean."

"You too, Nell. Y'all drive careful."

"Next time you pass to Lake Charles stop by," Estelle said.

"We will," Mom said. She hugged Estelle. "Every time we pass, Hardy wants to stop and hear you talk."

Estelle smiled at me watery-eyed.

"Would you say something in Cajun?" I asked.

"What you want to hear?"

"Anything."

Estelle put her hand to her mouth, cast her eyes down. "Look cross the road." She pointed her short, yellowish arm, and then the Cajun came smooth and lilting, the opposite of her rough-hewn appearance.

Mom nodded her head as Estelle spoke.

"What'd you say?"

"Your mama know."

I looked to Mom. "The trailers are pretty, but they're nothing but paper and wood. That's why I wouldn't have one."

An affirmative nod came from Estelle. Despite my misgivings, Mom knew Cajun.

As we walked by Estelle's car, I thought: It will never move again with her behind the wheel.

I pulled onto Highway 171. The sun was orange, half of it below the horizon. The sky was dusky gray. I turned on the headlights.

"When will you be home again from college?" Mom asked.

"Sometime in May."

Mom's cheeks flushed. "I'll put that surgery off till then."

It was night when we got home. I fed the cows in the dark.

BLESSINGS FROM A WOMAN OF THE GOOD GOD

Great-aunt Gertie, all four-foot six inches of her, tried to teach me to say God in Cajun.

Around nine on a July morning, we sat at her kitchen table, coffee fragranced the air. I feared stammering some awkward Cajun that Great-aunt Gertie would not comprehend, and worse, think me a fool for trying. As part of my linguistic self-education, I'd been listening to Father Jules Daigle's "Cajun Self-Taught" tapes and had learned a few set expressions such as, *Aujourd'hui c'est ma fête*—Today is my birthday; a saying infrequently needed. That July morning I would test myself. Great-aunt Gertie was to be my *Académie Française*.

I refused to use a memorized phrase. While visiting Mom that summer, she had taught me to say rabbit: *lapin* – LA-pah(n), which had been eating the tomatoes from her garden at dusk each day. From Father Daigle I knew how to say "at dusk" and "to eat," while Mom also taught me "garden," so I combined the two:

"*Á la brun la lapin manger leur jardin.*"

A nod and smile from Great-aunt Gertie before she corrected me:

"*Á la brun le lapin manger dans ma jardin.*"

Although Father Daigle was a priest, one word I had not heard on his tapes was God. I asked Great-aunt Gertie how to say it.

"*Le bon Dieu.*" The good God.

"Le bon do," I said.

"*Bon Dieu,*" she repeated, the "d" coming out soft as a "j," making a sloshing sound. I absorbed the sound, but had difficulty with it. I said "Do," too rough; I said "Jew," too soft.

To explain my limited Cajun, I told her I had been studying with Father Daigle's book and tapes. Great-aunt Gertie jumped up, hurried to the far wall of the living room, and pulled a plain maroon book from a shelf. "The little grandson got that for me last Christmas." She did not have Father Daigle's book that accompanies the tapes, but the dictionary. She opened it and a black and white glossy photo of the Father fell out. A thin-lipped man, shiny black hair parted down the center with graying edges. His black-frame glasses covered dark, sharp eyes.

On the tapes his personality is one of kindness, humility, and a penchant for not taking guff. He was in his eighties and nineties when he wrote the books and recorded the tapes. His eyesight was fading, and on occasion he skipped a word or read a page number incorrectly. But the sound engineer would gracefully catch Father Daigle, who quickly apologized, righted his mistake and moved on like a delightful grandfather.

Father Daigle was a parish priest east of Lake Charles in the small town of Welsh. Mom's first husband was a distant relative of his; third or fourth cousins from what I hear. After becoming a priest, Father Daigle learned seven more languages, including standard French. Toward the end of his life he began writing down the Cajun language, culminating with the tapes, accompanying book and dictionary: a permanent record of the Cajun language.

On his tapes, Father Daigle addresses the question: is Cajun bad French? His answer: if Cajun is considered bad French, then European French should be considered bad Latin. Cajun is often categorized as a dialect or a patois, both of which Father Daigle takes umbrage with. I concur with the good Father. American English, for example, began as British English and through other linguistic influences a new version was created. The same phenomenon occurred in Cajundom: French was brought by the Acadians and spiced with vocabulary from Africa, Spain, and Native Americans—a new tongue for a new reality. I propose that instead of using the term Cajun French, we simply call it Cajun. The fact that it is a type of French is almost universally understood, making the qualifier unnecessary. More importantly, the single term demonstrates our linguistic autonomy.

***

Before my summer visit, all I knew about Great-aunt Gertie was that she had married into the family through Great-uncle Gus, *Grandmére* Felice's baby brother. I'm told I met Great-aunt Gertie once as a toddler. In high school, just before Great-uncle Gus passed, she came by the house, and allegedly that's when I met her for the second time. But in 1998, I am certain I met her at Saint Michael's Church in Iowa (I-O-way) Louisiana, at the wedding of her baby girl. Extremely petite with short cropped hair graying around the ears, Great-aunt Gertie, clad in an emerald-colored dress, greeted me with a hug and familial friendliness that I'm not accustomed to receiving.

Great-aunt Gertie's lack of height struck me first; she was the first person I saw Mom lean down to hug. In July, I paid Great-aunt Gertie another visit and brought along Mom; they hadn't seen each other since the wedding.

"You remember when they was making that roll in the hair in 1940s?" Great-aunt Gertie asked.

"Yeah," Mom said.

"Well, I was the beautician and had to fix my stepmother's hair. She was not too glad when I got married. But my daddy said: 'I'm glad because I couldn't have give you a wedding.' We went to get the license. I was just 15 and we went to Lafayette. My husband was ten years older. The priest questioned him. My husband came back from the service and went back to school for his diploma, that's where I met him. We got married and went to get the clothes. My stepmother didn't want me to take too much."

"Was this Great-uncle Gus?" I asked.

"No. David Bellard from Church Point. We were married for twenty some odd years, then he died from a brain hemorrhage in '68.

"David, when he went in the service for World War II, was an interpreter. He went to Italy and knew French, English, and Italian. Now that was Cajun French, not the big French. But I guess you can talk with the big French. A lot of the Cajun soldiers went and come back and claimed they couldn't talk French anymore. Like my husband say: 'You don't forget that easy.'"

Until speaking with Great-aunt Gertie, I never knew Cajun men had served in World War II as French interpreters. In school, when we teach our children about war heroes, should these men be mentioned? They didn't do anything quite as impressive as the Navajo Code Encrypters, who only recently received their deserved recognition. All I know for certain is that these men were interpreters for American officers, and by wartime hero standards, they were just doing their jobs. But when you consider that for many of these men, the military was their first exposure to a totally Anglophone world, then their service seems extraordinary. Many had never before left their small communities in southwest Louisiana, and then they were transported to a far off military base with a drill sergeant barking commands in their faces. Some couldn't understand a word. Imagine the ridicule handed out by the drill sergeant, perhaps by fellow soldiers. The Cajun men felt tiny and shamed. No wonder many of them, once they mastered English and returned home, claimed to have forgotten Cajun.

"How'd you meet Great-uncle Gus?" I asked.

"We went to this little bar and we were a bunch of widows."

"And he picked you?" Mom asked.

"Someone else had eyed him to the table." Great-aunt Gertie whispered, "But I'm not gonna say who." Her voice picked up, "He danced with everybody at the table. So it went on, every week we'd go. Finally, me and my friend, she died now, we'd go together. Me and my friend, Gus bring us both to the thing and then one day she said: 'No. You go by yourself.' I was thirty-something-odd years old and that went on from there."

Great-aunt Gertie grew up in the middle of the 20th century, when Cajuns were encouraged to homogenize with Anglo America. "I was never ashamed of my French heritage. Long time ago when I was selling Avon, there was a lady in the trailer park on Broad Street in Lake Charles. She was from Quebec. She told me: 'I have never let nobody in my house. But you speak French.' We chatted a little while. In fact, I don't believe she bought nothing. But we had a nice little visit. It took me awhile to remember my French with her because I was raised speaking French, but then kinda got away from it. But me and my first husband always talked French and talked to the children in English."

"When we moved to Pensacola," Mom said, "I still had a bad French accent."

"Really? But did y'all talk French, y'all?"

"Yeah. Grandma Cummings, Mama, Aunt Laura, Aunt Florence...."

"You think Aunt Florence? I don't believe," Great-aunt Gertie said. "Or if she knew, she lost it. She married that German guy and I don't believe he talked French."

"When she was with Uncle Tom, she didn't talk French?" Mom asked.

"That's Marsalise you talking about."

"Who was Florence married to?"

"Bruce Stozel," Great-aunt Gertie said.

"Yeah, Uncle Bruce," Mom said. "No, he didn't talk French either. Maybe Aunt Florence knew just a little, because I remember her and Mama saying something in French. You know when they would talk about pregnant women, it was always in French. I asked Mama one day, how come y'all speak English a little bit, then y'all go to French. She said: 'It's something you shouldn't know.' Really, when I married, I didn't know anything about sex. I was just dumb. That's like when we started our periods. Mama didn't explain nothing. Oh, one morning I woke up and my bed was bloody and I was scared to death."

"Thought you were dying." A little laugh from Great-aunt Gertie.

"I went and told Mama I got blood everywhere. She said: 'Go let your older sister fix you up.' I said: 'But Mama, what's the matter?' She said: 'You'll understand.' She was ashamed to tell me."

"It wasn't spoken," Great-aunt Gertie said.

"I can't understand why they didn't," Mom said. "And I started so early, nine years old."

"I was twelve," Great-aunt Gertie said. "But the lady that washed the clothes noticed it, you know. Other than that, I was attending to myself and what I learned at school."

"They didn't tell us anything at school," Mom said. "I was in the bed crying I cramped so bad, and Grandma Cummings came to the house and she said to Mama: 'Ada, warm a plate and wrap it in a towel and put it on Nell's stomach.' I was tiny then, nothing but skin and bones. So Mama warmed up a platter in the oven and come and put it on my stomach. I passed clots and everything. Really, I should have went to a doctor."

"Normally it ran and if something happened, you died," Great-aunt Gertie said. "A sad situation. Not educated and didn't want to be educated, I guess."

"Daddy could read," Mom said, "and write a little bit. Mama couldn't do none. She could sign her name and that was it."

"My brother says we come from not too good of a family," Great-aunt Gertie said. "I told him, what we make of ourselves is what we are."

"That's it," Mom said.

"My mother had brought us to her old aunt and they had to go to the soup line; he said he remember that, and my mother died when he was five years old. But he said: 'See, I remember going to the soup line with my little bucket to get some food.' I didn't go because I was still on the bottle, I guess."

Great-aunt Gertie refilled our cups and began telling us about a documentary she had watched in Eunice at the Prairie Acadian Cultural Center on handfishing. "My first husband he fished like that. Him and his brothers, they all fished by hand."

"What do you mean, fish by hand?" I asked.

"Go along the walls, and if there is an old stick there, you go underneath and the fish is there. The catfish make a hole and back up in there. So David put his hand in there and when the catfish opens his mouth, he catches him through the gill and pull him out."

"What was your job when y'all went fishing?" I asked.

"I'd bring the sack. Me and my sister-in-law would follow them on the bank. They'd come back and put us our fish in the sack and then go back in the bayou."

"Did y'all eat and cook out there?" I asked.

"Only on Good Friday. We all jumped into a wagon: David's sister, the husband, and the mom. The poor mom, she would bring a bag of Irish potatoes and her grease to make sure she fried some potatoes for the children because they was going to be hungry if they didn't catch no fish. And then they made homemade pies and brought that. But then if we didn't catch no fish, we ate that and hightailed it back home. Whatever they fished we cleaned and cooked and ate in the woods. Fried fish and *coubillion*. It was very good. So much better outside. Cooked rice out there too. Put some bricks down to put you pots on and make a fire underneath. I still have my black pots."

***

Talking with Great-aunt Gertie and hearing of her handfishing exploits showed me how we Cajuns are folk of European stock who weren't afraid to adopt Native American ways. Handfishing, Native activity; Good Friday, Catholic holiday. Great-aunt Gertie is a child of this union, and though I am also part of it, I am removed from the union by time. My link is Great-aunt Gertie, the sparkle in her eyes as she tells her stories, her gay gestures, her rapid speech: all blessings from a woman of the Good God.

Mom and Grandpère Felice in the 1980s in front of the Felice family home.

Rendez-vous des Cadiens Prairie

Prairie Cajuns are Louisiana's cowboys. This area of southwest Louisiana is not all swamps and marshes. The land is low, consisting of pine forests and flat, grassy prairies perfect for cattle ranching. On a trail-ride in the late 1800s my *Grand-grandpère* Homer Felice met Miss Greenleaf, his future wife, when he stopped and requested water. I picture their encounter: on the outskirts of Broady Marsh, which I've been told by older relatives lies just east of Lake Charles, *Grand-grandpère* Felice and a few hundred head of cattle came through. Some family lore claims that *Grand-grandmère* was Cheyenne and that her family had fled imprisonment at a fort in Oklahoma. No historical records support this claim. The more probable explanation is that Miss Greenleaf was Coushatta—also known as the Koasati. Broady Marsh and *Feliceville* are roughly a half-hour drive from today's tribal headquarters of the Coushatta Nation in Elton, Louisiana.

When Homer met Miss Greenleaf she was a skinny teenager who drew a bucket of water from the well and brought it to him, a man in his late twenties or thirties. This all took place in front of the cypress cabin where Miss Greenleaf lived with her mother and father and most likely her siblings, though I'm not certain if she had any. In front of the cabin was her father's buggy, in which he made house calls, for he was a healer, perhaps a *traiteur*, and worked on Natives and non-Natives alike. Hearing the ruckus that a few hundred head of cattle made, Miss Greenleaf's father stepped out of the cabin to see a tall Prairie cowboy asking his daughter for a drink of water.

Grand-grandpère took the opportunity to rest his saddle sore backside and hopped off his horse. Out of respect, he spoke to Miss Greenleaf's father, and *Grand-grandpère* had to speak Cajun, the only language he knew. Miss Greenleaf's father, living in southwest Louisiana, probably also spoke Cajun or at least knew enough to understand that *Grand-grandpère* was thanking him for the water, the hospitality, and expressing desire for his daughter's hand in marriage. After drinking his fill, *Grand-grandpère* handed Miss Greenleaf the bucket and got back on his horse, but before leaving, he told her: "I'll be back for you." He drove the cattle to Lake Charles and sold them. He took that money and married Miss Greenleaf and bought six-hundred and fifty acres of virgin pine at a quarter an acre, the site today of *Feliceville*.

When I was eight I saw one black and white photo of Miss Greenleaf hanging in a bedroom in the Felice house. Memory tells me that she wore a buckskin dress, moccasins, and her hair hung to her waist in two braids. A couple of years ago I found a copy of a photograph of *Grand-grandmère*. The copy may have been of the same photograph that I had seen hanging on the wall in the Felice house; if it was, then my eight-year old mind and time created a totally different image. In the copy she wears a gingham dress, sits in front of a car holding a cat, her hair is pulled up on her head; she is a hard-faced woman without a smile. Miss Greenleaf's face and large nose resembles that of her son, my *grandpère* Kenney Felice, his lanky body a replica of hers. She passed in the 1930s and was only in early middle-age, but life on the Cajun Prairie took its toll.

With all this in mind, Mom and I entered the Prairie Acadian Cultural Center on a Saturday afternoon in the summer of 1999. The Cultural Center, which was built in 1991, faced West Park Avenue in Eunice, Louisiana, which is known as the "Cajun Prairie Capitol." In the center of the lobby were maps of all the continents decorated with brightly colored straight pins, representing the homes of all the visitors. Louisiana, of course, was pricked to death. All the other states had at least one pin, even Hawaii and Alaska, but the greatest concentration was in the Northeast and Midwest.

Canada had several pins, most of which, not surprisingly, were from the Maritimes and Quebec. In Europe, France commanded the most but was followed closely by England. French-speaking Africa also had quite a few pins. But what surprised me the most was Asia. The continent was not riddled with pins, but Japan and Korea had flurries of color, as well as Taiwan and Hong Kong. Folk came half-way around the world to visit this place, yet during my high school years I'd been living an hour from the Cultural Center and never heard of it until Great-aunt Gertie told me.

Bookshelves dominated the left wall of the lobby, with books and pamphlets ranging from French translations of "Evangeline" to historical and sociological accounts of Acadians, Cajuns, Creoles, and native tribes of Louisiana. At the end of the bookshelves were cookbooks, and across from them was the front desk, at which stood two Park Rangers in green militaristic-slacks and khaki shirts with a badge on their shoulders and name tags over their hearts. The man had a small black pony-tail protruding from the back of his head. His name tag read Domengeaux and he had a narrow, close cropped black beard, and his skin, slightly olive, shined softly, giving him a welcoming visage.

Ranger Woods also stood at the front desk and she told me to call her Ranger Claudia. She too had black hair, and her nose, prominent and proud, gave her a friendly countenance. A few other visitors, a mix of tourists and local older Cajun couples, walked around the Cultural Center, and Ranger Claudia went to help a lady find a specific cookbook while Ranger Domengeaux gave me a pin to put in the map. I had attended high school in DeRidder, Louisiana and Mom still lived there; however, at the time of the visit I was pursuing an MFA at the University of Memphis. Did I announce with my pin that I was a Louisiana insider or outsider? I squeezed my pin in amongst a half dozen others around DeRidder.

I stepped into the main exhibit room and *L'Historie* was immediately to my left with a wall map reminiscent of classical cartography entitled "The Acadian Migration." Red lines originating in France led to Maritime Canada, and from there more red lines led to the Caribbean before ending in south Louisiana.

Beneath the map was a timeline which began with 1604, the year the Acadians left western France and settled in Canada—creating *L'Acadie*. The term *Acadie* is believed to come from the *Mi'kmaq*'s suffix *–akadie*, meaning "a place of abundance," and while there the Acadians intermarried with the *Mi'kmaq*. The British were outnumbered by the Acadians, who had been there for five generations and refused to swear allegiance to the King of England or take up arms for him. The *Mi'kmaq* were sworn enemies of the British, and not wanting to risk insulting their neighbors and in-laws gave the Acadians all the more reason to remain neutral.

Neutrality or not, in 1765 the British exiled the Acadians, in what is called *les Grand Dérangement*—The Great Disturbance. Perhaps demonstrating our sense of humor, *dérangement* means "diarrhea," and I have heard that *les Grand Dérangement* caused us to cease using the French word, *drapeau*, for "flag." In Cajun a *drapeau* is a "diaper," and we use the English word "flag." To explain how this change in connotation occurred, I have heard two possibilities. Theory #1: since France did not defend us from Great Britain, we thought of their flag as a diaper. Theory #2: this was our response when the British asked us to swear allegiance to the Union Jack. #2 sounds the most likely. Old World or New World, an opportunity to insult the British flag and Crown was not going to be passed up by the French. During *les Grand Dérangement*, the Acadians could bring only what they could carry, and families were purposely split up, mama on one barely seaworthy ship, papa on another, and the children on still another. The British lured the Acadian men to a phony public meeting and detained them there, leaving only the women and children at the homes, making them easy to round up.

In their 161 years in *L'Acadie*, the Acadians developed their own culture, one not based on royalty and wealth like feudal France. From the *Mi'kmaq* they developed egalitarian ideas, and once exiled, they looked to preserve their way of life, and after ten years of dispersion a group of 281 Acadians arrived in New Orleans. The Creole aristocracy there, which consisted of royals and wealthy persons from France where the Acadians would have been their peasants, looked down on these new arrivals. Language was part of the problem. While Creole aristocrats and Acadians were French, they spoke with different accents and pronunciations. Like a Boston attorney and a Mississippi sharecropper conversing, each knew the other's place.

The Acadians solved their strained relationship with their French brethren by requesting land from the Spanish governor, who badly needed settlers for the colony. Louisiana, with its swamps, mosquitoes, and oppressive heat, did not invite settlers. While some Acadians settled along the bayous outside of New Orleans, most of the Acadians saw the isolated Attakapas district of southwest Louisiana as the ideal locale to recreate *L'Acadie*. This area is separated from New Orleans and the rest of southeast Louisiana by the Atchafalaya Basin, America's largest wetland and swamp. The Basin made it difficult for outsiders to get to the Acadians. And if they were difficult to reach, then it would be even harder for another government to remove them.

Separated from mainstream America geographically and linguistically, when the Civil War began Cajuns were thrown into a struggle which most knew nothing about. Most Cajuns were subsistence farmers, who had no stake in the plantation system. Louisiana, however, was a Confederate state and needed every able-bodied man they could round up to serve as soldiers. Cajun men often hunted and trapped, giving them experience with weapons and knowledge of the terrain, which came in handy during their military service and distinguished some of them from their comrades.

Despite some serving commendably, Cajuns, by and large, were coerced participants in the Civil War, and desertion rates were high. It was not uncommon for the army to bring a few hundred Cajun men to a camp and have only a fraction of that number remaining in a few days. The men hit the woods and marshes at night, and many stayed in them for the duration of the War. *Grand-grandpère* Homer Felice escaped to the marsh around the Atchafalaya River and waited out the War there for two years. For meat he killed rabbits, dug a hole and built a fire, cut the meat into strips and smoked it. He carried this fresh jerky in a pouch and had food for awhile, supplementing the berries and other vegetation he picked, along with the fish he speared with a small sharpened branch or caught by hand. While many Southerners proudly recall their ancestors' roles in the Civil War, I am glad to say that *Grand-grandpère* deserted and refused to fight. His refusal places him and other Cajuns in a unique position as white Southerners; and it should, considering that Anglo-slave owners in Louisiana didn't want their slaves associating with my ancestors, fearing that our "laziness" would infect them. Interestingly, as whites in American culture, we found ourselves, during the time of slavery, socially beneath the enslaved.

The marriage between my great-grandparents always fascinated me because they came from such different backgrounds: one Native American and the other possibly an ethnic Spaniard Francophone in an Anglo nation. Maybe their commonality came from their marginalized positions. Both knew what it was like to be removed from their homes. I wonder if they shared stories? When *Grand-grandpère* told of his time in the marsh, did Miss Greenelaf counter with tales of her people leaving their homeland in Alabama due to European encroachment, and after settling in Louisiana, dealing with Cajun settlers. Exile and adversity were the soil out of which their love grew, and I am one of the limbs that sprouted from their tree.

Next entry on the timeline: in 1968 CODOFIL—Council for the Development of French in Louisiana—was founded by Congressman James Domengeaux. One of the first activities conducted by CODOFIL was to bring in teachers from Belgium, France, and Quebec to teach French to south Louisiana's children. James Domengeaux was proud to be French, but made it known that he was not Cajun, and therefore the French that was taught in the schools was European. Many Cajuns criticized CODOFIL for this and believed it insulting. Bringing French back to the schools was well-intended, but Cajun children should have been taught our culture's language.

Today CODOFIL is headed by a Cajun, Warren Perrin, an attorney who operates the Acadian Museum in Erath. He has made vigorous efforts to end ethnic slurs against Cajuns, particularly stamping out the use of "coonass."Although there is debate about the term's origin, one explanation is that it developed during slavery. Cajuns at that time were not enslaved, but since they were some of the first European settlers to Louisiana, they often had the choicest land; however, when the Anglo-Americans moved in, they wanted those same lands for their plantations, thereby forcing many Cajuns to relocate. The Anglos couldn't enslave us and thusly they found us useless, and deemed us lower than a coon's ass.

The word's origins aside, "coonass" is also problematic because many older Cajuns from Mom's generation view the term as an insult. As a child, I was reprimanded by her on the few occasions I said it. Back then, I thought Mom was angered because the term has a curse word in it. In the latter part of the 20th century, younger Cajuns began embracing the word. Bumper stickers reading "RCA"—Registered CoonAss—are frequent sights. While I'm part of the generation that has made the word its own, I'm torn about it. If "coonass" did begin during slavery, then the word not only insults Cajuns, but also African Americans. When I think of the word in that vein, I do not embrace it, and part of me wants it exterminated. However, there are Cajuns who use the word as a means of controlling their identity, much as some African Americans have done with the "N" word.

When someone calls me a "coonass" my response depends on the context. Case in point: A classmate in the MFA program at the University of Memphis threw a party and some of her Boston friends attended. When we were introduced, my classmate told them that I was Cajun, to which one responded: "You're a coonass."

"No. I'm Cajun."

"I used to work at a casino in Mississippi, and the people from Louisiana said that's what you call yourselves."

"Some of us do call ourselves that, but I'd prefer you not call me that."

Our conversation ended with him screwing up his face and walking off. I did not appreciate his gall at telling me that "we" call ourselves "coonasses." Perhaps his comment was an attempt at bonding; perhaps I was too thin skinned.

I have family members who revel in the word. Most of these folks are men, and for them, "coonass" expresses machismo and connotes one who is strong and hard-working. When these relatives say "coonass" I am not angered. But should I be? Am I wrong to overlook my family's use of a word that angers me when a stranger says it? Even if the word did begin as an ethnic slur, the word's meaning has evolved with younger Cajuns putting a positive spin on it, and if the word is now affirmative, does that supersede its negative origin?

While the merits of Warren Perrin's attempt to eradicate "coonass" are debatable, he is doing an activity that I unabashedly approve of: taking on the British Crown. He found a petition that two Acadians brought to King George III after the British-French War was over. The Acadian petition asked King George III to formally declare *les Grand Dérangment* finished. Only problem: his Highness never read it. Perrin did, and slapped an amendment on it so he couldn't be accused of presenting an untimely request, and in 1990 he personally delivered it to the British government through a consular office in America. Perrin's amendment goes a step further than the petition and asks that a physical marker be built recognizing that the Acadian deportation is over; for until *les Grand Dérangment* is declared over all Acadians living in Canada are illegal aliens, and when Cajuns visit they are in violation of Canadian law. When I learned of this in 1999, I longed to stand on the shores of Nova Scotia where our Acadian ancestors had been forced into ships, take the sea-air deep into my lungs, and enjoy the bliss of breaking an unjust law.

I am happy to report that my law-breaking dream is now no longer necessary. Although it took 13 years, on December 9th, 2003, a Royal Proclamation was signed decreeing July 28th as the annual Day of Commemoration of the Acadian Deportation. *Merci beaucoup,* Mr. Perrin.

1986, the last entry on the timeline, read: "Cajun Chic. Interest in all things Cajun, but especially food and music, sweeps the nation." I didn't see any extension of the timeline to include the 21st century. But I'm curious as to what events may punctuate our future. Hopefully, in the year 2240 there won't be an entry that reads: "Last Self-Acknowledging Cajun Dies." I like to hope there would be mention of great Cajun accomplishments as well as positive evolution to our way of life. Change is inevitable for any living organism, but we need to make sure that we, not others, are the ones picking and choosing what remains and what changes.

To the right of the timeline was *La Langage* exhibit. I walked under an arch and tripped an infrared sensor that set off a tape of Cajun conversations that were recorded on the streets and at local establishments in small towns throughout south Louisiana. A map on the wall in this section entitled *Les Voyages des Acadiens* showed the routes the language took from France to Canada, Africa, and the Caribbean on its way to Louisiana. In the bottom corner of the map was a condensed explanation of how Acadian French originated in west-central France. When they left for the New World, these Acadians brought their peasant speech with them and remained isolated from European French while in *L'Acadie*. After they arrived in Louisiana, Acadian French evolved again, taking on aspects of Spanish such as the lightly trilled "r," and vocabulary from Spanish, Native Americans, Africans, and English, to create the Cajun language.

Cajun has nine words that mean "to annoy": *gêner, nuire, agacer, tracassér, emmerder, embêter, empester, taquiner, tourmenter*. Having nine different words expressing annoyance illustrates peasant honesty: if we don't like you, we'll let you know. But the language is also affectionate. Many older Cajuns end every greeting with *cher*, "dear" or "beloved." Pet names between lovers abound too: *jolie*, "pretty"; *catin*, "doll"; *jolie catin*, "pretty doll." *'Tite monde"* is one term of affection that doesn't translate well. Literally it means "little world." When used by a husband or boyfriend, however, it means "little one."

Despite the criticism Cajun receives for being outlandish, what you hear spoken is a democratized, welcoming language, usually extending an invitation of food and coffee, or something a little stronger. True, drinking is an activity for which Cajuns are notorious, but just as the Irish aren't all drunks, neither are we. I find it interesting that the word for drunk is one of the most guttural words in the language: *Chaqué*, CHAW-kay, sounding like a Klingon in Star Trek; perfect example of sound reinforcing meaning.

***

All this talk of Acadians and Cajuns can be confusing. Here is the difference: to be a Cajun, one doesn't have to be Acadian. Acadians were simply the first European settlers to south Louisiana and developed into the dominant local culture. But in the 1800s, other European immigrants, mainly the Irish and Germans, came into the region and married Acadian women After the 1800s, Acadians and these new immigrants alike all came to be called Cajuns.

For my particular ethnic make-up, I consulted Aunt Lacy, my oldest living relative at the time. "Daddy's Mama was Indian," she said across the phone line in a strained voice—an enlarged heart affected her breathing. "She was Cheyenne."

"Cheyenne in southwest Louisiana?" I asked.

"They were originally from Oklahoma, and had escaped from a fort up there. They traveled around setting up camp and hunting, and kept coming south. The hunting in Broady Marsh must have been good 'cause they stayed there and built a cabin. Her maiden name was Greenleaf and her daddy was a doctor and he'd ride round in a buggy to people's homes." Broady Marsh is only twenty miles or so south of *Feliceville*.

While it is possible that the family story of *Grand-grandmère* being Cheyenne may be true, it does not fit the historical accounts. Of course, one's family history can go against "official" history, but the location of Broady Marsh on the periphery of the Coushatta tribe's lands seems compelling. Originally from Alabama, they moved west and arrived in southwest Louisiana in the 1800s. When Indian Territory—current day Oklahoma—was established, some members of the tribe moved there but most eventually returned. I wonder if this is possibly where the story of *Grand-grandmère's* Oklahoma origins came from? Also, while in Indian Territory, could her family have married into the Cheyenne, and hence that is the tribe that she is affiliated with in family stories?

Aunt Lacy continued: "Daddy's daddy was French from Hecker, Louisiana"—which is right beside Broady Marsh.

When Aunt Lacy said that *Grand-grandpère* was French, I cannot assume that the descriptor means his ethnicity. Felice is both a French and Spanish surname, and with the close proximity of *Feliceville* to Texas—as well as Spain controlling Louisiana for years—there is a good chance that some of my ancestors simply crossed the Sabine River, or perhaps we are descended from a Spanish soldier. Spanish surnames such as Castille, Ortego, Aguillar, Segura are Cajun surnames. One reason it is difficult to discover *Grand-grandpère's* ethnicity is because he was an orphan. I don't know if the adoptive parents were named Felice, or if they give him that name as a good portent—it means "happy." I have not been told what led to him being orphaned, but perhaps he was the product of a Spanish father from Texas or Spain and a Cajun mother. Did the Spanish father dessert his family? If so, was the task of raising a child by herself too great for the mother and she gave up her child in order to ensure that he would be taken care of? Or did the era's strict moral codes make her a Cajun Hester Prynne, and the stigma made her give up her child? Or did the Cajun Prairie simply take the mother's life?

Although I am unable to know the exact context of *Grand-grandpère's* adoption, I am inclined to believe that the Felices are part Spanish. Uncles and male cousins have dark heads of hair and thick mustaches—the stereotypical Latino look. I believe the Anglo genes of the Jones family kept these features from being passed to me

Aunt Lacy filled me in on *Grandmère* Felice's make-up: "Mama's mama was French and her maiden name was Peliqan. Her daddy was Dutch and Irish and came over here from Ireland and worked cutting timber round Iowa, Louisiana."

My conversation with Aunt Lacy, for the most part, answered my question of our ethnic make-up. Now I know that through Mom I am part French, Irish, Dutch, Cheyenne or Coushatta, and probably Spanish. Although I am still not certain if I have any Acadian in me, these other ethnicities combine to create me: a newly identified Cajun.

***

I entered *La Musique*, and it was fitting that the song "*Jolie Blond*" came on, for this song about a pretty blonde leaving her husband for another man and fleeing to Texas is the unofficial Cajun anthem. Of course, my parents' story is the song come to life, except Dad the Texan took Mom to Florida. *La Musique* was in the left corner of the main room with a glass enclosure separating it from *La Langage*. Handmade cigar-box fiddles were inside the glass enclosure. The fiddle, not the accordion, was the original Acadian instrument. During the exile Acadians did not bring any instruments with them to Louisiana, and once they settled in Louisiana they began making cigar-box fiddles. Irish and German immigrants taught the Acadians ways to improve the instruments and to build concert quality violins.

Also in the glass case was an accordion, the lead instrument in modern Cajun music. German Jews brought the accordion to south Louisiana in 1880. After World War I, the single-row button accordion gained popularity and became the accordion of choice and still is in most Cajun bands. Squeezing out two-steps and waltzes was time well spent, for during World War II the accordion supply from Germany was cut off, and Cajuns began building their own, and are still doing so.

Two lesser known Cajun instruments are *le 'tit fer*—little iron triangle—and *le frottoir*—scrubboard. Both are rhythm instruments. *Le 'tit fer* was originally made from the tines of hay rakes, while *le frottoir* was originally just a simple washboard. *Le 'tit fer* is still used today by some Cajun bands, usually by ones who play the more traditional acoustic style. *Le frottoir* plays a lesser role in modern Cajun music, but is a mainstay in zydeco, the black Creole music similar to Cajun music. No longer a simple washboard, today *le frottoir* is a corrugated steel-vest worn over the musician's shoulders.

Cajun music and zydeco are often confused by outsiders who hear an accordion and assume the two are the same. They are musical cousins, sharing similar influences that range from German, Spanish, Afro-Caribbean, Anglo-American, and, of course, French. Cajun music and zydeco are for dancing, which is why both maintain waltz and two-step time. Zydeco, however, utilizes syncopation, stressing the rhythmical "weak" note—one-TWO one-TWO instead of the standard ONE-two

ONE-two. Zydeco, furthermore, has its feet in the blues and R&B, so it is often electric and funky.

The diversity of influences on Cajun music is seen in the names of our most accomplished musicians. Dennis McGee, considered by many the best Cajun fiddle player of the 20th century, didn't even know his last name was Irish. "McGee, that's a French name," he once explained. "I don't know anyone named McGee who doesn't speak French." Another Irish-Cajun, Nathan Abshire was an outstanding accordionist, and his most famous song, "Pine Grove Blues," is a rocking two-step with a call and response between him and the fiddle player. Nathan asks: *"Ma Negresse, où toi t'es hier soir?"*—My black lady, where were you last night? Acadians are represented as well, with the late legendary accordionists Iry Lejeune and Austin Pitre, and contemporary violinist Michael Doucet.

***

The handfishing video that Great-aunt Gertie recommended was about a half-hour long, and it depicted a fun family outing similar to the one she had spoken of. After the video, a music demonstration was put on in the same room. A small carpeted stage, with a two feet rise, sat against the far wall. The floor of the room was wooden, light tan in color with diamond-designs. The chairs were close to the low stage and gave me the feeling of being in someone's living room. The informal tone of the presentation added to the cozy vibe.

On the stage sat two older men, the musical volunteers. Kern Fruge, a short, bullishly-built man, played a small single-row button accordion, light golden in color, which rested in his lap. In his younger days he had been the sheriff in Eunice, but now was retired. Kern sat in the middle of the stage and to his left was George Sonnier, with his long legs crossed and the fiddle on his shoulder. To the right of them, sat Ranger Claudia with an acoustic guitar, and at her feet was Ranger Domengeaux with a pair of spoons. They asked for requests and Mom spoke up: "'Poor Hobo.' You never hear anyone play it anymore."

Ranger Claudia looked to Kern. "Do you know it?"

A few hesitant squeezes of the accordion, and with each one Kern's face softened, until a toe-tapping tempo emanated and he said: "It's been a while since I played it. I thought I forgot it." "Poor Hobo," or *"Pauvre* Hobo," was *Grandpère* Felice's favorite song. Mom has told me how he'd take the battery out of his Plymouth and put it in the radio on Friday and Saturday nights to listen to the Grand Ole Opry and Cajun music programs. *Grandpère* played the radio full tilt, but every time *"Pauvre* Hobo" came on, he somehow got a lot more juice out of the battery. When *Grandpère* wasn't dancing in the living room, he sat in front of the blaring radio, head down, elbows on knees, feet patting time.

Once the music started, two Cajun couples from the edge of the audience rose and danced. Present were eight older Cajun couples and three Northerners. *"Pauvre Hobo"* is a two-step, so the couples held each other as if waltzing but performed an upbeat dance around the floor. I leaned to my left and asked Mom to dance. She loves to dance, but since her knee operations, it has not been an activity that she can engage in often. You couldn't tell, however, by the way she and I slid smoothly across the floor.

I don't know if *Grandpère* Felice liked *"Pauvre Hobo"* because of its toe-tapping time, or because in addition to cutting timber for Grandfather Jones' sawmill he worked on the train and had frequent contact with rail riders. Some evenings, *Grandpère* came walking home with a man. *Grandpère* would feed the hobo and let him stay a night, but only a night. The next day the man accompanied him back to the train.

No hobos were present that day in the Cultural Center, but I danced with Mom to a song that she and *Grandpère* Felice used to dance to. Culture passed, generations bridged. Since I was small, when playing a Cajun record, Mom always grabbed me and danced at least one song. While enjoyable, dancing in a museum dedicated to preserving our culture felt a little uncanny. Preservation, I am all for. But it frightens me that it comes from the government, and I'm a little sad, for this means that many of us may not be passing on our unique ways ourselves.

❊

As a child, the yell that goes *"Iii-eeee"* always stood out in my mind. The word is spelled *a-i-l* and it means "garlic," so don't ask me why it is yelled. I've asked and so far no one knows, but I suppose it could have something to do with our love for seasoning, or possibly due to our contact with local tribes. We imitated their yells and cries, incorporating them into our music, with a Francofied twist. Or, maybe we perform the yell because it is a fun way to let off a lot of steam.

Prior to finishing the music demonstration, Ranger Claudia gave us lessons on how to properly perform the yell to the Cajun standard *"J'etais au bal"*—"I Went to the Dance." At the end of the lines is when you do the yell, filling the gap between verses or to signal a solo. No solos were performed when we did our yell, because Ranger Claudia had us practice it *a cappella* a few times first. "The trick is to be loud, but on key," she said after our first attempt, which sounded little better than a pack of basset hounds with sore throats. Poor sound aside, I performed a yell my ancestors created. Greedily, I relished this experience.

On our second attempt, most of us were on. Me, I yelled not so loud on the second try, wanting to get an ear full of everyone else. Perfect pitch came from in front and behind me. Satisfied with our second *a cappella* effort, they played *"J'etais au bal"* two times through, giving us six yells, and by the last one we could have been mistaken for an out of work joyous choir.

"Give yourselves a hand," Ranger Claudia said.

We did and then gave her and Kern and George and Ranger Domengeaux one in return.

"In a few minutes," Ranger Claudia announced as everyone stood, "we'll have a cooking demonstration in the kitchen." Many of the older folk rose slowly, taking time to loosen joints from sitting and the ones who had danced had to get their fatigued legs to working. It seemed it was going to take awhile for all of us to make it to the cooking demonstration, so I had time for more exploration.

The Cultural Center's exhibits on history, language and music were understandable, but along the back wall of the Center was an exhibit dedicated to *le Joie de Vivre*. This exhibit made me especially proud to be Cajun, for in a world in which people, beyond all else, want to be happy we are known to enjoy life.

Dancing, by far, is the most famous Cajun pastime, so no wonder dancing couples, circa 1950s, were wall-papered behind this exhibit. The men in the picture wore suits or sports coats and the dark-haired women sported fashionable dresses, many with sweaters and light jackets. A tradition that only ceased in the mid-20th century was *le Bal de Maison*; otherwise called a *fais do-do*, "go to sleep," because all attended the dances, including little ones who were laid to rest in the host family's bedrooms. For a family to announce they were holding a *bal*, they usually sent a *bougre*, a young chap, on horseback; he rode by every house waving a red flag. Families came from miles, for this was pre-dancehall, and the beverages in the house were water or coffee. Alcohol had to be found outdoors, and gamblers were banished to the barn. On the Cajun prairie, chicken and sausage gumbo was commonly served to the guests at midnight. A *bal de maison* ended when the musicians walked to the yard, fired pistol shots into the air, and loudly proclaimed: *"le bal est fini!"*

Mom was born in 1935 and grew up with such dances. She spoke of moving the furniture—a sofa and a few chairs—out to the front yard and pouring salt on the wooden floor (a smoothed floor a bonus). Neighbors came from all over *Feliceville*, some walking, some on horseback, families in a buggy or on a sled. A few fortunate folk drove a car. The music was provided by neighbors and family as well. A neighbor four houses down named Cleveland Crochet played a heavenly fiddle. *Les bal de maisons* introduced Uncle Dub to music. I imagine him as a boy listening to the musicians, the violin and accordion seeping into his mind, his fingers mimicking those of the players, until one day he had his own instruments.

Mom's stories of *les bal de maisons* offered some differences from the Cultural Center's exhibit. Alcohol was not allowed on my grandparents' property, so one could not even find a drink in their barn. *Grandpère* was the son of a moonshiner, yet he was a teetotaler. Perhaps his father making his living from the sale of alcohol made *Grandpère* see it solely as a source of income. Or perhaps through some of his father's customers *Grandpère* had seen the negative side of drinking.

Other differences for the *bal de maison* at *chez* Felice was that they did not end with gunfire, nor did the *bal* always end at midnight. When I first heard these differences I thought perhaps that my family was not "authentic"; in an effort to understand my Cajun identity, I wanted my family's practices to conform to the "official" history. Arriving late to my cultural heritage, I already felt displaced and hearing anything about my family that did not fit the established historical narrative made me feel like a pretender. But a culture is not monolithic. My experiences growing up in Florida, for example, were different from a person who was raised in Minnesota, but these differences do not make either one of us any less American. The same is true for my Cajun half of the family: their ways illustrate just how diverse the culture is.

In *Le Joie de Vivre* exhibit, special attention was given to horses, which were brought in from Spanish Texas, where they were plentiful and cheap, so even subsistence Cajun farmers and ranchers could afford a few. (Perhaps a horse deal is what brought my Spanish ancestor to Louisiana?) The most famous Cajun equestrian activity today is horse racing, which was brought to us by Americans in the 1780s. There are tracks in Lafayette and Vinton, a little town near the Texas line, and the most popular type of race features quarter-horses. Before organized tracks, we still found a way to race: the Cajun Straight Race. At first, these only took place at social gatherings, which sometimes included church. The men would send the women and children in for mass and race on the church grounds, making for many a pissed-off priest.

Horses, of course, were and are still not merely for work and racing. They are essential to *Le Courir de Mardi Gras*—the Running of the Mardi Gras. Cajun Mardi Gras is different from that held in New Orleans. Traditional Cajun Mardi Gras does not consist of bead throwing and parades, but of masked and costumed riders on horseback making their way through the country side, house to house, on a begging quest collecting the makings for a communal gumbo to be shared in the evening. In the past, this was to ensure that all members of the community enjoyed one big meal in the dead of winter when supplies in isolated communities were running low, and of course Mardi Gras gave them all one last day of fun before Lent.

The riders' begging quest begins at sunrise and they make it back to town in early afternoon, exhibiting intoxicated jubilance. Many riders return to town standing in the saddle, or with a foot on two horses, or riding facing the wrong direction. Once the riders return with the alms, cooking commences. Giant pots suspended above outdoor fires cook the gumbo. Each will have a different type: chicken and sausage, duck, guinea. While the gumbos cook, bands play and folk dance. Usually the gumbo is cooked either at a town park or the downtown area is blocked off, creating a huge street dance which ends at midnight, the beginning of Lent. And for those who are devout Catholics, that means no more dancing and drinking for forty days until Easter.

I never celebrated Mardi Gras until I was an undergraduate at LSU in the mid 1990s, and this was in New Orleans with friends. For information on Cajun Mardi Gras, I again relied upon Mom. During her first marriage, she always participated in Mardi Gras. One year she was washing breakfast dishes and through the kitchen window she saw some masked riders in her chicken yard, where they grabbed a fat Rhode Island Red hen. She stopped washing dishes and went to the back door.

"Don't take all my fat hens, no," Mom said.

"We just want this one," one of the riders said, climbing back on his horse. "Your family coming to the gumbo this evening?"

"Oh yeah. We'll be there."

These masked riders were fellow rice farmers from nearby, and they were so casual and neighborly that they didn't have the *Capitane* approach the house and ask if they could beg for alms. In past years, however, a whole band of riders came, circling the house and banging on the walls. According to Mom, of my four sisters, Rebecca and Barbara were the easiest to scare, and when the riders made their commotion, they hid under their beds. Catherine and Margaret were braver and they took part in the games of being "stolen" and "whipped" by the riders. After the riders came by the house in the morning, that afternoon Mom placed the girls in the car along with a few pounds of sausage and a fifty pound bag of rice and drove to the park in the town of Jennings. Amidst the revelry, people would discuss what their Lenten sacrifice would be. The married men, Mom said, always joked that they were giving up marital relations. This always engendered laughter, and sometime ribbing, for if that man had claimed the same sacrifice the year before and his wife had a baby that fall, then the other men accused him of not having kept his sacrifice.

***

The crowd from the music demonstration straggled in to the kitchen. There were a dozen rows of folding chairs and Mom sat in the end seat on the front row. A long armed man parked a wheelchair just behind my left shoulder. In the chair sat a gray haired woman, robust in size, but it seemed age had chipped away a bit of her alacrity. The man, while his hair was solid gray, was not as old as the lady. He had large, dark eyes, but they did not seem out of place on his face. In fact, they were his greatest physical compliment, testifying to what I assumed was a kind heart.

Cory McCauley, the cook, had a pencil-thin mustache, wore a bright white shirt, and announced that he was making crawfish *ètouffèe*. One complaint about *ètouffèe* is that it takes too much time to prepare. Cory demonstrated a method of lightly frying the crawfish tails prior to cooking that cuts the time down to twenty minutes, which was good because it was getting close to dinner time and none of us could wait to get a bite of the crawfish tails, which are the size of shrimp but with a sweet taste closer to lobster. For the *ètouffèe* —"smothered"—they are covered in a creamy gravy seasoned with garlic and onions and served, as most of our dishes are, over rice.

Cory talked us through the preparation, and all heads were cast at a 45 degree angle, watching the mirror above him as he melted butter, fried down the crawfish tails, sautéed the onions, bell peppers, and celery. True to his word that this recipe was a time saver, Cory finished in about ten minutes. A line formed for the stove, where we received a plastic cup of *ètouffèe*, only enough to tantalize. I and others, such as the long-armed man, went back for seconds and thirds. But none went past thirds; we had to save some for Rangers Claudia and Domengeaux.

With eating came more talk and folk began sitting closer together, some still spooning bites, others holding empty cups. Over our second cup of *ètouffèe*, I learned the long-armed man's name was Ivy Joe Doucet and the woman in the wheelchair was his step-mother. It was her 84th birthday, and he'd taken her out for the evening. They both lived in Rayne, a small town south of Eunice; him at home and her, due to a stroke, in a retirement home.

Mr. Doucet and Mom originally struck up conversation, and when I was introduced, the tag "he's in college" was added. Mr. Doucet looked at me and with a heavy Cajun accent said: "An education is better than an oil well. It won't ever go dry." He asked: "*Parler-vous françaíse?*"

"No, sir. But I'm learning."

He nodded with the strained look of a disappointed grandfather.

Mr. Doucet pushed his step-mother out of the kitchen in search of some more food, because "they only give a man enough to tease him here." Others seemed to have the same thing in mind, including Mom. I was not hungry for more food, but for knowledge.

I went straight to *L'Huile*—Oil—exhibit. Oil was discovered in a Cajun's rice field in 1901, twenty miles from the site of the Cultural Center. Ever since, oil has been a blessing and curse. After that first well, oil companies poured into south Louisiana looking for another strike. Many Cajuns who owned land were enticed into letting the oil companies drill on their property. Most of these landowners, however, only received a fraction of the money that the oil company made from their land.

While the oil workers who came in from Texas and Oklahoma didn't think much of Cajun men, they loved our dark-eyed beauties. When an outsider, rich after a week's work in the oilfields and cranked up on beer, danced with a Cajun woman, it wasn't long before he was asked to step outside. On a plaque mounted in front of black and white photos of grimy, tired oil field workers, one Texan recalled: "Saturdays we'd be let out from the drilling crew, clean up, and go to the Cajun dance. I was nineteen and full of it. Get in but a dance or two, then I'd have to go outside and fight."

This account fits the image I was raised with of Louisiana oil towns. By the time I came along in the 1970s, however, land drilling was all but played out and off-shore rigs dominated as they still do. Towns along the coast where men left to go offshore for the oil rigs were notorious, with names like Cameron, Houma, Morgan City, and Cut-off. These were places where a brawl seemed only a breath away.

A large black and white cut-out stood in front of the wall and depicted Louisiana's modern oilfields: off-shore derricks, with a crew, most sitting and wearing lifejackets, enjoying a smoke break. Their clothes are smeared black, their faces gaunt, and their bodies exhausted. As time went on in the 20th century, Cajun men who knew the land and waterways proved indispensable to the oil companies, who, after initially believing we were too stupid to work the expensive machinery, began to employ us. In order to work on the oil rigs, however, Cajun men had to speak English to their bosses, which contributed to the decline and ridicule of the Cajun language in the 20th century.

Oil was something tangible and of the earth, but religion and ethereality are also parts of Cajun culture, and proof of this is seen in *L'Eglise* exhibit. Prior to the 20th century, medical services were few and far between on southwest Louisiana's prairies, and *les traiteurs,* Cajun healers who combined Catholicism with folk remedies, filled the need. *On va demander au Bon Dieu*—we will ask God—was how most cures began. After that initial invocation, a *traiteur* whispered secret prayers and made the sign of the cross over the patient's affected body part to remove the pain or illness. A cross drawn in the wrong direction, however, only made the patient worse. The effectiveness of a *traiteur* was not solely dependent on faith, for they also learned many herbal remedies from local Native Americans. These included smoke from tobacco to cure ear aches and applying spider webs to stop bleeding. Aunt Lacy mentioned that Great-grandmother's father had been a doctor, and this makes me wonder if he was one of the Native Americans providing traditional knowledge of medicinal herbs and plants to *traiteurs*. Or was he a *traiteur*? I like to believe he was and interpret Aunt Lacy's use of "doctor" as interchangeable with *traiteur*.

Inside *L'Eglise* exhibit was a thread necklace with an alligator's tooth for a charm. This was given to children to ease the pain of teething. Adult patients were often made to wear a *corde de neuf noeud*—string of nine knots—until it fell off, and when it did, it took the patient's disease with it. Sunstroke in south Louisiana's hot, humid summers was easy to incur for ranchers and farmers, but *les traiteurs* had a cure for that too. They covered the patient's head with a red cloth and passed a pan of water over it, drawing the fever out.

Until I visited the Cultural Center, I had never heard of *traiteurs*. As a little girl, Mom knew of them but was never treated by one. As a child in Florida, I remember folk asking Mom if she knew voodoo. This question was only posed after they learned that she was Cajun. Mom did not know voodoo nor do I know any Cajuns who do. I suppose the *traiteurs* and their mystical ways may have contributed to this false impression along with most outsiders confusing Cajundom with New Orleans.

One telling sign that I have returned to south Louisiana are all the statues of the Virgin Mary in the front of homes. Many are protected from the elements by a white grotto, usually a bathtub sunk halfway into the ground. Statues of Mary occur in other areas of the country with high concentrations of Catholics, but Her statues are a little more special to Acadians/Cajuns because "Our Lady of the Assumption" is our patron saint, made so in 1938 by Pope Pius XI. Despite our veneration of Mary, Cajuns are notoriously cross with clergy, priests being the butt of many of our verbal jabs. Case in point: a common Cajun greeting is *"Comment ça va?"* and an idiomatic response is *"Mieux que ça et les prêtres seraient jaloux!"*—Any better than this and the priests would be jealous. In addition, a priest in pre-twentieth century southwest Louisiana always ran the risk of being forced from his parsonage. These ousting of priests became so numerous that it has been noted that Cajuns are "the most Protestant of Catholics."

A few banished priests aside, we do enjoy religious holidays. Our Easter celebrations are fun and begin a week prior with Palm Sunday—*Dimanche des Rameaux*. After

Easter mass, the fun really begins with *poquer*, a game in which two eggs are hit together. If you crack your adversary's egg, you win, get it as your spoil, and move on to another opponent until only one contestant remains with an egg. Since a hard shell is a plus, geese and guinea eggs are preferred. Mom told me stories of how my older brothers often won these contests with such eggs.

I have often referenced Mom's stories, my original link to the culture, and paradoxically her stories made me feel a part of and apart from our culture. Hearing them introduced me to experiences, allowed me to imagine them, but since I had to rely on my imagination, it meant these experiences were not visceral. Likewise, this visit to the Cultural Center brought me closer to our culture, while pointing out aspects from which I am distanced. I feel as if I am trying to overcompensate for late cultural awareness by wanting to have my hand in every facet of our culture. I must realize that even if I had been raised in the bosom of our culture that would have been an impossible task.

***

I stood in the center of the room, scanning all of the exhibits, and absorbed the information. Some of these things I knew, such as the language, music, and religion, but horse racing and the negative effects the oil industry had on our culture, I had not known. Seeing these exhibits triggered a memory, one I've had since early childhood. I remember knowing from a small child that Mom's family, my Cajun relatives and ancestors, had a hard life ranching and farming. The Cultural Center reaffirmed this and made me understand that though I sometimes long for old-time Cajun life, it was brutal. And, truthfully, was probably more than my soft-under-worked-twenty-first-century-body could handle. Surviving, however, is something I do not have to do; I have to make sure and not forget what my ancestors endured to get me and other young Cajuns to this point.

The Cultural Center gives us no excuses for being ignorant of our past, and that was why I was disappointed that young Cajuns were not present. The attending older Cajuns, many who lived the life portrayed in the Center, are not the future.

They are important as passers of our culture, yet a passer needs a receiver. Without generational advancement, we as a people stagnate, culturally wither, and—inevitably—die. After trying for most of the twentieth century to homogenize us, Cajuns and our ways were not supposed to have lasted this long, but we have, and after enduring external forces, now we must survive self-decay.

The Wealthiest Accordion Player

Cajun music is one our culture's richest commodities, and accordion player Cory McCauley is the wealthiest man I know. I arrived at his home—ten minutes outside of Mamou—where he and Alexie, his five year old son, both sporting straw hats, planted cantaloupes and okra. Lisa, his wife, is a French teacher at Mamou Junior High and had to attend a meeting at school that day. After shaking hands, I made a failed attempt to correctly pronounce Alexie's name, for it came out roughly as Alex-ee not Ahleck-say. The garden was beside the house and separated from the front yard by a waist-high wire fence. Eggplants and sprouting tomatoes, in two rows about six feet long, were freshly planted in the dry ground.

"We need rain, yes," Cory said, pouring water for his cantaloupes.

No rain for the past few weeks, but that day a wall of dark clouds in the south lingered deliciously.

"Always plant in the mud," Cory said and dug a small hole with his hand, unwrapped the damp newspaper from the plant's roots and placed a tiny cantaloupe sprout in the ground. Alexie, in shorts and knee-high black rubber-boots, squatted next to his papa, taking instructions in Cajun. I was glad to see a member of my generation—Cory was thirty-one—speak our language, and I was a little envious that I couldn't understand everything being said; but most importantly, Alexie did.

Cory wore small, round glasses, giving him the visage of a philosopher, while his closely cropped brown hair spoke of orderliness. Due to his cooking demonstration at the Prairie Acadian Cultural Center, I thought he was a chef, but Cory corrected me: cooking is a hobby, music is his passion.

After the two rows of cantaloupes and okra were planted and Alexie, hoe in hand, vanquished a lone cluster of grass at the edge of the garden, we went into the house, stepping into a screened gallery on the backside of the structure that opened onto a large combined kitchen and dining area with a varnished wood floor. A pair of rocking chairs sat left of the kitchen table. It was a quarter to noon and Cory prepared two hot dogs for Alexie, who sat across from me at the round kitchen table squirting ketchup on both sides of the buns.

"Most men round here cook," Cory said, sitting to my left. "There is kind of a tradition of men getting together, usually on a weeknight. My dad wasn't into cooking until after he retired because he was a farmer and when he finished in the fields, he was tired and didn't want to mess with it. But I had some cousins who took their time to cook. Seems like they would always try to out spice each other, you know.

"Another kind of event is what is called a *boucherie*, which is becoming less and less common as fewer people raise hogs. At that instance, you had men and women dividing the work; the men would be outside slaughtering the hogs, scraping the hair off the skin, cutting the meat into different pieces. The women would be in an outdoor kitchen grinding the meat, cutting onions, cooking rice and innards to go in the boudin. And the kids would be in between that. My job was to cut the crackling meat—the fat and the skin. That was pretty safe, and you can't hardly do it wrong."

"We raised hogs when I was in high school," I said. "And when we butchered in the morning, that day for lunch we always made backbone stew."

"That must be kind of a universal tradition. We did the same thing," Cory said. "Towards the spring and summer it's good to barbecue. This area has a certain way of barbecuing that is different from other places in Louisiana and from other places in the South. Generally we use cuts of meat, like pork steaks, rather than barbecuing a roast and then cutting it into slices. My family has a sauce that is a very light pink, and is used for basting the meat. It's not sweet like you find in, say, Memphis."

Cory explained how his family ended up in south Louisiana. "The first McCauley to come here was named Patrick and he came from Ireland to Virginia, and he married a woman there, then came to Louisiana and settled near Bayou Chicot. He later moved to Chataignier in about 1770, during the time when Louisiana was owned by Spain. So he was Irish, married to an American, was living in Louisiana under Spanish rule, and was a member of the Opelousas Militia fighting for the Americans against the British in the Revolution. He was really an international type of person!

"My last name is Irish and that was mixed with some German, some Desoehotel, and Manuel, which is probably Spanish. My mother was a Fontenot, her mother was a Miller, German again. Some Reed, which is Irish again. None of my family's background is Acadian, which is quite common in Evangeline parish."

Also ironic, given that the parish was named after Longfellow's poem recounting the Acadian exile.

I asked Cory about the genesis of his musical career.

"I started playing the accordion when I was a teenager in Soileau. I had a neighbor who played, and he really got me interested in it. Not on purpose. He really kind of discouraged me on the exterior. But I was just fascinated by the instrument and the music, so I continued to fight it."

Speaking of his accordion mentor, Cory's pace slowed and his tone gained solemnity. "He lived at the corner of the highway and parish road, where we lived. He had a store and was there all the time. A lot of times he was practicing, because he didn't have all that much business."

Hadley Fontenot taught Cory the accordion, and to truly appreciate who is teacher was, know that Hadley Fontenot played for the first family of Cajun music: the Balfa Brothers. When you want to hear unadulterated Cajun music with nothing but a triangle, two fiddles, an acoustic guitar and accordion accompanied by mournfully jubilant wails, you listen to the Balfa Brothers.

Like many Cajun bands during the time of the Second World War, the Balfa Brothers had only a string band, but when soldiers came home, the accordion made a triumphant return to the music. Cory elaborated, "People started dusting off their accordions and some of these players, like Mr. Hadley, who had not been in a band, all of a sudden had work again. Dewy Balfa told me the story, and said he went to his dad. 'Pop,' Dewey says, 'we really need to get an accordion player for our band, but we don't know who.' His dad thought for a while and says, 'Oh yeah, I know. Hadley!'

"Sure enough, they went to see him and at that time Mr. Hadley lived straight back in the woods. Dewey told me they got out there and Hadley was trying to farm in those hills and piney woods and wasn't doing any good. To make ends meet, Mr. Hadley would go to the woods and cut small pine trees. Then he'd go to town and collect people's waste oil from their engines. He built a trough back at his place out of some old fifty-five gallon drums, and he would take the bark off these trees and put them in the trough, pour that oil on them, then light some pine knots underneath the trough to boil the oil so it would penetrate the wood. Then he'd take the trees and sell them for fence-posts. Talk about some hard work.

"When Dewey and his brothers got there, they told him they wanted him to play with them, and at that time Mr. Hadley didn't even have an accordion because he'd sold his. But when they told him what they wanted, he sat down on his porch and just cried he was so happy.

"They started playing dances, eight or nine a week. Twice on Sunday, twice on Saturday. Just about every night of the week at different places. Did that for years. Mr. Hadley moved out of there and kind of prospered; opened his store. By the time I knew him in the 70s he was established in Soileau with his store and his music.

"At the time that I was in my teens and started wanting to learn how to play, Mr. Hadley had been all over the world with his accordion, and I knew doctors and lawyers in town who had never traveled outside of the state. It was just amazing to me that someone with very little education could accomplish these things."

Cory pulled out his accordion—a shiny sandy-color with gilded ruffles. "This is an old tune that nobody ever plays. It was recorded by Amede Breaux in 1934. It's a really interesting song. There's a lot of country and western influence in Cajun music, and that's been going on since the 30s with Texas swing. But before that, there was influence from popular big band music and jazz. This is an example of that, because it uses the name of an old jazz standard, 'Tiger Rag.'" A wash cloth on his knee and the accordion on it, Cory, right foot patting time, played a jumping beat with short, quickly repeated bars and a fearsome rhythm. "I used to be a trumpet player in high school, and I approach the accordion kind of like the trumpet because the sound is similar: real brassy and quick. The Cajun accordion is not like the regular accordion; it is very strong and powerful!"

Alexie sat in his papa's lap while I snapped two photos. The first one was proud Papa with son in lap; the second, son and accordion in lap. The clouds from earlier were black and low, hovering above the house, and a cooling gust of wind hit us in the face as Cory and Alexie walked me to my car. I shook their hands and had another go at pronouncing Alexie's name, doing somewhat better this time. As I backed out of the drive way, thunder rumbled. Providence, sweet Providence.

Cory's Crawfish Ètouffèe

Ingredients:
1 stick butter
3 medium white onions, chopped
1 medium bell pepper, chopped
Half cup chopped celery
2 lbs. cleaned crawfish tails
6 large cloves of garlic, minced
1 cup green onion tops, chopped
Half cup of parsley, chopped
3 cups of water, approximately
2 teaspoons cornstarch
Salt and pepper to taste

In a large heavy sauce pan or Dutch oven, melt butter and add crawfish tails. Fry down the crawfish tails over medium heat. When butter turns red, remove crawfish tails and sauté onions, bell pepper, and celery until vegetables are tender.

All this time add water and cornstarch. Amount of water can be varied according to thickness of gravy desired. Season with salt and pepper to taste. Cook mixture down to desired thickness. Add crawfish tails, green onions, garlic, and parsley. Simmer about 20 minutes. Serve over rice.

Lunch avec Monsieur Doucet

"He came on two horses." *Monsieur* Doucet held up two fingers, gnarled and knotty from a lifetime of sharecropping and working off-shore, as he told me about his great-grandfather. "A pack horse and a saddle horse. He came to the Richard community. They liked him, and he stayed. For a long time he had the name John Texas. But that wasn't his family's name. He picked up the name Richard. I don't know if he didn't want anybody to know where he was at...that's all I was told. John Texas died 1930 November the 19th. He married a Venable. He had, I don't know, how many children. Four or five, I guess. My grandfather was the oldest. I'm the oldest grandchild. I was born in 1930, around Richard Community, a place called Pointe Noire."

I had met Mns. Doucet at the Prairie Acadian Cultural Center in Eunice a couple of weeks earlier, and before he left the Cultural Center, I had asked him if I could visit. He said he welcomed the company and gave me his address in Rayne.

We sat facing each other at Mns. Doucet's kitchen table—white and oblong with a red and white checkered table cloth—and on the stove top behind him sat a deer roast that'd been simmering in brown gravy since sunrise. It was now a quarter to noon. Lima beans and rice cooked while a bowl of beets sat in the middle of the table. Mns. Doucet got a pitcher of homemade Zatarain's root beer out of the refrigerator and poured us each a glass into Cypress Bayou Casino coin cups.

Mns. Doucet checked the deer roast; fragrant steam rose around his face. The kitchen and living room was an open area, great for visiting and large families, with a highly varnished wood floor. Under the coffee table's glass top were saints' cards and others depicting Mary and Jesus. The Catholic presence was strong in the house, but not onerous. I turned back toward the table as Mns. Doucet resumed his seat.

"I worked at the Evangeline bakery for three years, then went to work in Crowley doing construction, building the rice mill and the rice bends (tall cylindrical structures used to dry the rice before loading it in trucks or rail cars). I was one of the last ones working construction there. Most of the workers were from Kansas, that cowboy town Dodge City. They wanted me to go with them and keep working, but I didn't have enough money to go back and forth. After that I went back to the bakery for a little while. Then I worked oil rigs out of Jennings until 1967. Then a friend of mine came here one day when I was working the bakery and the oil rigs.

"My wife had just been operated on and I had to put my son in the hospital seven times in that year for his prostate. They couldn't find out what was wrong with him. My friend told me I was working too many hours. I told him I have to make it. He got me an application to work off-shore, and I did that for eighteen years, retired in 1983. Doctor said my back was just over worked." This is evident whenever Mns. Doucet first stands: his shoulders hunch for a few moments until he takes some steps and straightens up.

After his first two marriages ended with his wives' passing, in 1995 Mns. Doucet married Bulah Hicham-Bottom. "She was kind of in my mama's family. One day she called me and said she would like to come visit me. I was living by myself in Rayne and she was living in Church Point with only her Social Security for income. After we met she said she would like to stay with me. We married and combined our benefits. Now she's in the old folks home, real bad diabetes."

***

Mns. Doucet called Mr. Patin and Cowboy into the house. They sat in the garage when I arrived, and as I entered Mns. Doucet's house, they stared at me wondering: who was this stranger visiting our friend? The two men now flanked us at the table, Mr. Patin on the right and Cowboy to my left. Earlier, before Mns. Doucet told me about his great-grandfather, he leaned to me and whispered, "Said he going to the overpass." Mns. Doucet's voice broke. "My friend, no. Not when I got an extra bedroom." He was speaking about Cowboy who had recently lost his house and possessions—including a 150 year old violin—to a fire, and was looking at sleeping under I-10's overpass north of Rayne.

Mns. Doucet got plates out of the cupboard and told us to help ourselves. I waited at the table until Mr. Patin and Cowboy served themselves, then, with a little prompting from Mns. Doucet, I fixed a plate. I spooned up two small mounds of rice and covered them with the brown gravy along with a few slices of meat; next to that I put a light green dollop of lima beans to round out my lunch. I didn't touch the beets on the table, although the others did. The meat was tender, my spoon sharp enough to cut it, and the brown gravy was seasoned perfectly, leaving no need to add salt or pepper; the same was true of the beans. For dessert we had banana-pudding-flavored ice cream.

Mr. Patin, a short man of slight yet sturdy build, is a house painter and painted Mns. Doucet's house in 1996; the two struck up a friendship. Both men enjoy attending the horse races at Evangeline Downs on the outskirts of Lafayette. Mr. Patin has poor night vision and with his work night races are the only ones he can attend, so Mns. Doucet drives them in his new Dodge pickup.

The earlier tension I felt from Mr. Patin and Cowboy greatly diminished once I explained that I had family in Rayne, an aunt, uncle and a slew of cousins. But it was Mom's maiden name, Felice, that endeared me to them. This newfound acceptance opened them up and Cowboy quickly shared with me that he had been a professional musician in the 1960s and 1970s, playing with local legend Happy Fats, who had an afternoon radio program.

Mr. Patin did not converse as freely. He did, however, speak Cajun with Cowboy and Mns. Doucet. The rapid, smooth sounds of our mother tongue fired around the table, and while I only plucked out snatches of the conversation, Mns. Doucet sagaciously stopped periodically and filled me in on what was being said. He even took time to help me with pronunciation, and when I repeated something he taught me, Mr. Patin smiled.

Along with the Cajun lesson, Mns. Doucet took great care explaining that Cajun was not the same as the French spoken in France, which is referred to as standard French, a label I can accept. Growing up, though, I heard standard French called "real" French, a label I cannot tolerate. Granted our pronunciation is not the same, we have many idiomatic expressions and words that don't exist in France, but we passed our language down by word of mouth, and had Native Americans, Africans, and new arrivals from Europe learning our French, so of course a new version of the old language developed. Case in point: my great-grandfather Cummings—my grandmother's father—came from Ireland, married a Cajun woman who demanded that he speak her language, and thus he spoke French with an Irish brogue.

After lunch Cowboy went to his bedroom for a nap and Mr. Patin returned to his house, a block away, to do the same. Mns. Doucet told him to come back that afternoon for coffee. Mr. Patin said he would and we shook hands, his eyes no longer glaring, but glowing warmly.

"Don't let me bother your routine, Mns. Doucet. If you want to nap, I can go."

He shook his head side to side. "The last year I miss a lot of naps. My wife, they cut her leg off last August." His voice trembled, eyes watered, and he ground the heel of his palm into his eyes. "Almost lost her."

***

A week later I called Mns. Doucet from my apartment in Memphis. He'd been to the doctor, and on the way home had been rear-ended.

"I don't know what I'm going to do, Hardy. Ought to bring myself to the retirement home and be with my wife."

"You don't need to do that, *Monsieur* Doucet. Your truck'll be repaired. It'll run like new."

"I don't know. Ought to bring myself to the retirement home. Die with my wife."

"Don't talk like that. Please, Mns. Doucet."

"It's the truth, yeah. Me, I got to go, Hardy."

I called back two weeks later and was happy to hear his voice on the other end. He told me his truck was out of the shop; Cowboy had found work and his own place, and that evening Mr. Patin was coming over and they were going to the horse races.

Glad to hear the good news, Mns. Doucet.

Cajun Dreams

Fred Charlie spoke Cajun to me even before I met him in his gift shop and recording studio in Eunice. A few years back he made a tape entitled "You Can Speak Cajun French," which I bought through a catalog and have used in concert with Father Daigle's tapes. Fred's store is around the corner from the Prairie Acadian Cultural Center and on my initial visit to the Cultural Center I went by there. When I walked in Fred greeted me in English, and his raspy voice sounded familiar, but I couldn't place it. His voice had an almost dream-like quality. And, quite possibly, I could have heard it in one; I was in the habit of putting on the tape when I lay down at night. I told Fred this, and he said, "I bet I put you right to sleep."

Fred wore black jeans with tan cowboy boots and a cowboy shirt with horizontal lines—white, turquoise, teal, purple, black—breaking away from each other. Fred stood six feet, maybe a little taller, with raven hair, beard, and eyes. We sat in front of the soundboard in the studio sound room. Fred sat tall and erect in his chair, but dark-rings shadowed his eyes. That morning he went on the air for his weekly radio show on KJJB 105.5, simulcast on KEUN 1490 AM, at seven and the show airs until noon.

With all that was done to eradicate our language, I wondered how the tape came to be.

Fred cleared his throat and began: "There are a lot of tourists who come to south Louisiana and they gave me the idea because they were looking for something to pick up on. But then I started thinking there are a lot of people here that would like to be able to speak French but just don't have a way of doing it. The tape was really basic: numbers, days of the week, addressing people, counting money, parts of the body. We used a French dictionary to write our notes. I'd say it my way, then we'd write down. My wife stayed on me, because a lot of times I wanted to say it like they would in France. She said, 'No. I want you to say it like you say it,' because that's how we speak here."

Fred definitely did that. I noticed he pronounced the days of the week slightly different from Father Daigle. The difference, however, does not make one unintelligible from the other. Pronunciations vary within in the same language. People in Boston don't sound like people in Birmingham, but they're all speaking American English. And Father Daigle and Fred were speaking Cajun.

Fred spoke more about his tape: "The most flattering experience was when a teacher from New York came in one day with a bus tour. She asked me who I was, so I introduced myself. She went back out on the street, and came back in with all of her kids from the tour bus. One of the kids saw the tape in the rack. And she said, 'That's the tape I use to teach y'all French. Now class, I'd like for you to meet the man that's on the tape.' It was pretty neat that they were using my tape, somebody that can't read or write French."

The language Mom was punished for speaking at school is now taught to New York City children. Quite a happy surprise. I do not expect the New York children to become fluent. Most will probably not continue with the language after that class is finished. But children who most likely had never known for certain what a Cajun was have been exposed to our language.

While New York children are learning our language, Fred Charlie told me some disturbing news about his four grown children: "None of them speak French. They understand some of it. And that's the sad part about it, because there's a generation or two that got stuck in that gap where for a long time it wasn't passed on. I was never whipped for speaking

French on the school grounds, but we were encouraged not to. My parents and grandparents probably were actually spanked for speaking French. And I can understand where the teachers were coming from. Here you have some educated people that have a degree in teaching and you're handed twenty first-graders that speak French. So you have to teach them a whole new language and get them prepared for life."

The government said that one cannot simply speak French and function in America, but Fred told another story: "Even as of today, and I'm fifty-one, I still do business in French. I was a painting-contractor for twenty-five years here in Eunice and I got more jobs because I spoke French. It's a closeness and a trust people have with each other. In my painting business I know a lot of times I was high bidder. But because I sat down and drank coffee with these old people and just kinda shot the breeze in French with them, I'd get the job. When we were growing up our parents and grandparents, if somebody spoke English, they'd say, "*Ça c'est les Amercain,*' There's those Americans, and here we were the Cajuns."

Closeness is what I'm looking for as I learn Cajun. I cannot wait until the day arrives when I can express myself fully through the language of my ancestors, allowing me to understand how earlier generations of my family perceived the world.

Cajun bands, by and large, sing in French. Even, in some cases, if they don't know the language. But I was curious about Fred Charlie's band, one in which the members did know Cajun. Did they speak the language when they weren't on stage? "We speak French," he said, "but not all the time. It's more Frenglish. We use it in and out. Pretty much like how Cajuns speak. You meet two Cajuns on a street corner and they can start talking in French, and if they speak for ten minutes, they have changed from French to English maybe twenty-five or thirty times. You go to a certain point and it's just automatic. I went to France in 1990 and a lot of the French people think that we were brilliant because our brain was working in both languages. When I switch from one to another, a lot of it's because I get stumped on a word. Anyway I speak fluent French, sometimes there are some words that you just can't think of right away. When I get stuck, I jump to

English. Then when I feel comfortable again, I switch back to French."

Due to the fact that Cajun uses many English words, we are often criticized by other Francophones who want us to retain pure French. Fred had another view of the situation. "I find that French in France has incorporated more English in some senses than we have. I was totally disappointed when I got there. They gave us a car and I couldn't wait to get to the first stop sign where it would say '*Arrêt*'. But it had 'Stop.' So I asked one of the guides and he said, 'We don't put out everything in French.' They call it 'stop,' only they put a little French to it."

France provided Fred with the opportunity to hear old words that have been lost during our time in the New World. "I enjoy that part of France," Fred said, "where I can speak and hear words that I haven't heard since I was a kid. It's amazing how many words you get in the habit of not using. My program on Saturday mornings, we try to have an old French word that hasn't been used in a long time. One time we asked how do you say 'unless' in French. '*Ormis*' is one of the oldest French words, and we stumped everybody. The phone rang off the hook, people giving us all kinds of different sayings. I said, 'No. I use that one too.' It's not that it's incorrect, I just wanted to see if they knew that old word. I caught it in here in the studio. One night this little girl was recording and she called her song "*Tee Vas Pas Me Courtiser Ormis Parler Française!*"—You Can't Court Me Unless You Speak French. But when I heard it, and it's a beautiful old French word, I said, 'Man, I hadn't heard that in a long time.' So the next Saturday, I put it on the show and people were calling and calling and talking about it. So we brought that one back to life."

Translations of song lyrics in liner notes have been a godsend for me, giving me mini-Cajun lessons, and enabling me to finally understand the songs. The CDs I own that were recorded by Fred, however, don't have song translations.

"They want us to put it in French and English to try and bring back the French," he said. "I feel it's ok to do it, if you want to do it. Cajun is a language that is basically phonetically written, and you get into trouble fast, because some of these guys read French and if you do it phonetically it's not gonna be spelled right. They may come back and get all over you because you misspelled something. It's misspelled to him, because he's reading French. But it's not misspelled to us because we wrote it as we sound it. Some of the old songs we do that have been spelled in French already, we follow that. If I misspell something, I blame the guy I took it from." A quick laugh and he cleared his throat. "We've proven that the language can survive, because we've been here three hundred years and can still speak French. That's a pretty good track record."

Being able to read and write our language is a beneficial practice, and as an author my sentiments are biased. A downside I can possibly foresee is the risk of losing idiomatic expressions common only to spoken Cajun. Such expressions can only be passed on by word of mouth, and undoubtedly idioms will not vanish all at once; future generations of fluent Cajuns will do as our ancestors and create their own lingo. Mom gave me that very advice: "Once you can speak Cajun, you'll start making up your own expressions."

In the summer of 1999, during that first visit to Fred's, he had just released his first CD entitled "*En Travers Les Annees*"—Through The Years. The first song on it is titled "*Trois Cent Annees*"—Three Hundred Years. "I wanted to write something about the Franco-Fete," he said. In 1999, Franco-Fete was a yearlong celebration all over Louisiana honoring the three hundred years of French settlement in the state. "Once it was written, then I found out there was a contest going on for songs about the culture. I went ahead and entered it and came out in the top ten. "*Trois Cent Annees*" says, 'We've been here for three hundred years, our grandfathers came here and found this place for us to live. And after three hundred years, we can still speak French. And the second verse goes into the government tried to stop us, but we didn't listen. Again, three hundred years and we still speak French.'"

Helping to carry the language and music to future generations of Cajuns and non-Cajuns alike, I wanted to get Fred's take on where he saw our culture headed. "Twenty, thirty years ago we were in bad shape. We're probably close to the top, but it's going to take us a long time to peak out. It's growing and not just with Cajun people. People throughout the United States and abroad get into this Cajun thing and just love it. The Cajun people have recognized that we are like a commodity and there are things to sell. Not sell yourself, but we can sell our culture because they think we're so different."

Selling our culture while we are ignorant of it shows a lack of respect and equals making a dishonest dollar. I do not worry about Fred doing this. He lived through our dark period and now prospers. With him and other older Cajuns leading the way, younger ones such as me will have no problem bringing our culture to the world.

Cajuns have rarely been strong economically, but in the latter part of the twentieth century we made strides with folk such as Fred Charlie. Others, who are not Cajun and know little or nothing about us, have profited from us, but it is good to see that we are now taking the initiative. Unlike most entrepreneurs, Fred is cultural as well as economic, protecting our ways as he profits from them. As long as Fred and other cognizant Cajuns are the ones doling out our culture to the rest of the world, we control our image, and can paint accurate pictures. Responsibility: if we as a whole assume charge of our culture, whatever aspects that are lost will be our fault. A weighty position, indeed, but one I relish. And after hearing what Fred had to say about the popularity of his language tape, it is a position I am certain all Cajuns can nourish.

Dry Gumbo

While a student in the MFA program at the University of Memphis from 1998 to 2000, every Wednesday afternoon from four to six, WEVL Volunteer Radio 90 provided me with my Cajun music and zydeco fix. The show is called 'House Bayou' and is hosted by Susan, who does an excellent job of mixing traditional and contemporary styles as well as explaining that the two musical styles, while similar, are different.

At first it was strange hearing a Cajun music program hosted with a monotone Midwest accent—on air Susan said she was from Chicago. Back in Louisiana most such shows are conducted in Cajun. Occasionally Susan has a Cajun man sit in with her; he translates titles and lyrics, and speaks a little Cajun on air. Images of Louisiana: flooded rice fields and rusty pump-houses, dense sugar cane fields, and mud-splattered logging trucks all came to me when I heard our language. The images the DJ engendered didn't surprise me, but the sadness I felt, knowing if I went outside I would not be there hammered home how much Louisiana had become a part of me.

Another good thing Susan does is point out that Cajuns live predominantly in southwest Louisiana, not New Orleans. In Memphis, most people assume I am from the Crescent City. If the inquisitor doesn't have the foggiest notion where Lake Charles—the largest city near DeRidder—is, I begin working my way east, Lafayette; still no, Baton Rouge; still no, New Orleans. Those two words, invariably, engender a Yes. Then I tell them I am a four hour drive west of the Big Easy.

One Sunday afternoon in Memphis I had lunch with the family of a retired Baptist minister. The meal consisted of the usual weekend fare: grilled chicken, baked beans, a green salad, bread, and sweet tea. I earned this invitation from the minister's daughter, a co-worker of mine at that time, and over our meal, the mother asked me if I was Cajun—her daughter had told them I was from Louisiana. I said yes, whereupon the mother threw her hands in the air and ran into the kitchen. "Here," she said, and set a tiny bottle of hot sauce in front of me. "That ought to make you feel at home."

The hot sauce had 'Louisiana' in bold letters in the shape of peppers with flames flicking the edges. For all the attention brought to the Bayou State by the label, on the back of the bottle was a New Jersey address. I had never had New Jersey hot sauce, but seeing as how the Reverend had laid off the seasonings, I figured I couldn't make the chicken any worse.

After lunch, I helped with the dishes, and the mother, as I handed her a dirty platter, said: "You don't sound like you'd be Cajun."

I am aggravated by such comments, and sometimes I fantasize of speaking with a Cajun accent. I have on occasion while out in Memphis, laid on an accent as thick as a spicy jambalaya. That is not what I want to do in order to "sound Cajun," and I have stopped doing it. Folk will simply have to take my word that I am Cajun. But these doubters give me another reason to learn my mother tongue. When folk doubt I am telling them the truth, I could simply *parle Cadien*.

Despite being doubted in Memphis, the greatest compliment concerning my accent occurred here. Mom called one afternoon just as I was about to go to class. "What y'all doing in there tonight?" she asked.

"They read one of my stories and are gonna tell me what they thought about it." Laughter filled my ear. "What's so funny?" I asked.

"You sounded just like a-Frenchman."

Unlike the times I'd put on a fake accent, that time when I had opened my mouth, the accent flowed without pretense. But whatever Cajun accent I have is due to Mom, so it's fitting that she pointed it out to me.

***

My two years in Memphis have allowed me to see what others think about us, and, yes, a lot of it does revolve around swamps and what we won't eat, which in most folks' estimation ain't too much. As necessary as it was to find out how others view us, I knew that I must return to Louisiana and speak to other Cajuns. My research began awkwardly; I didn't really know what I was looking for. All I knew was that I wanted a taste of the old Cajun life, the one from the early twentieth century, the one I had not been part of.

During my research, I made it a point not to talk to Cajun intellectuals—no, that is not a paradox. I didn't want folk who, although they are Cajun, had years of academic training. Speaking with them would have been an interesting approach and would have definitely shown us in a different light from TV and movies. Taking into consideration images the media uses for us, likewise, I didn't want to speak with eccentric marsh hermits. Again, I don't doubt that knowledge would have abounded from such individuals, but I wanted to talk with Cajuns that the media forgot.

I ended up speaking to quite a few musicians. That is partly my own bias; I love music and have a fascination for folk who communicate without words. Music is our most distinguishing outward feature, for in every squeeze of the accordion and cry of the fiddle lives our personality—jubilant and heart-broken— for all to hear. Lacking much of a written history, music is our literature, keeping our legends, folktales, and most importantly, our language alive.

In the past, negative stereotypes had kept me from admitting I was Cajun. I was afraid what others would think of me, and I didn't even realize that not all stereotypes about us are negative. Who wouldn't want to be considered generous and hospitable? In my travels I learned that Cajun generosity and hospitality are alive and well. Mns. Doucet served me a homemade lunch and even opened his house to me for a weekend stay that I unfortunately had to refuse. All of this, he offered after knowing me for only a few hours: old time values brought into the new millennium.

Laziness is our worst stereotype. I'm sure, if I had looked, I could have found some who fit it, either sitting on the river bank with a fishing pole and a beer, or in a dark bar in the middle of the day. But I didn't look for those folk, and neither did I seek out industrious beavers. Only after talking with Mns. Doucet did I learn that he walked thirty miles one-way to work at the bakery, and held down that job at night while he worked in the oil fields during the day. Lazy? No. Exceptional? Possibly. Cajun? Yes.

A disheartening moment during my research was when Great-aunt Gertie told me "the French we use is not the real French." Old folk such as she and Estelle Richard and Mns. Doucet still see our French as inferior to that of Europe, and worse, they view it as not a real language. Well, the language is definitely real every time they or any other Cajun speaks it. It conveys the value system of our peasant ancestry who refused to give up their autonomy, their religion, their language: their way of life. Qualities to cherish and continue. The language was real in the 18th and 19th century for our Acadian ancestors and the immigrants who settled south Louisiana and adopted the vernacular, and it was real for Cajuns of the twentieth century, even after being sequestered to the house.

Luckily, younger Cajuns such as Cory McCauley see our language for what it truly is: a valuable commodity. While we can't change the attitude of the older generation, we can make sure and not plant the same seeds of shame in the next generation's mind. When I began this book, I worried I was too American to be Cajun. Now I know that an aspect of Cajun identity means to be a part of the American tapestry. Estelle Richard, Great-aunt Gertie, Mns. Doucet, Fred Charlie were raised in a predominately French world, with minor influences from the rest of America, while Cory, his son Alexie, and myself have been raised with a full assault of American culture through education and TV. Yet we are all thoroughly Cajun.

But there is more to being Cajun than merely a patch in the American tapestry. We are a quilt unto ourselves, made up of our own patches. One patch is religion, and in the heart of the

Protestant South, we have remained a strong Catholic presence with a Catholicism that like its followers is tied to the land, the seasons, the harvests. That is why every year the priests of south Louisiana bless the rice and sugar cane fields before any farmer plants a seed and the shrimp boats before one net is dragged. And why Mom's first husband annually gave his first two-hundred pounds of harvested rice as a tithe.

Today, many young Cajuns are either non-practicing Catholics, or have simply left the Church entirely. Almost all of my seven older half-siblings have done the latter. After centuries of helping to shape Cajun culture, the Church seems to be playing a smaller role. Can Cajun identity survive without the Church's influence? Or with a lessening Catholic influence, will our ways remain unique from the rest of America, yet different from the old-time Cajun life? A pickle for the People of the Good God.

The largest and thinnest patch of the Cajun quilt is abject poverty. In the past it set us under the wealthier Anglos in the area and placed us shoulder to shoulder with African Americans. Since African Americans and we were poor and different from the Anglos, we were both the butts of their jokes. More damaging, the Anglos also tried to convince us that we were inferior; first by trying to prove that we were physically different from them, which failed the tests of science. Then they wanted to prove that we were less intelligent than other whites, using our lack of English and formal education as evidence supporting their claims. That was unfair, and reinforces the fact that one culture can't simply apply its standards in judging another.

We were not innocent, either. Anglo-Americans failed our criteria. They viewed us as indolent, we saw them as aggressive and materialistic; they viewed us as dance-happy drunkards, we saw them as sour and dour.

Why am I so adamant about keeping our culture alive? After all, what would the world really miss if our rural ways passed? Or would the world even notice we were gone? I view Cajun culture with the same zeal a survivor of a near-death experience does life. I was dead to my Cajun identity for the first twenty-five years of my life, and I want to spend the rest of my years living it, exploring it . . . loving it!

The encounter in that Iowa City bar was fortuitous. But what if I hadn't gone to Iowa? Maybe I would still simply see myself as a beach-lover from Florida, while Mom and the Felices would still be mysterious. Perhaps my desire to learn a ridiculed language would not exist; nor would my infatuation for the land and folk of south Louisiana. I would have turned my back on my culture, on my past—on who I am.

Writing this book taught me that Cajun culture resembles its most famous dish: gumbo. The foundation of a good gumbo is a roux; the Acadians are our cultural roux, providing the language and religion, while the Spanish, Germans, Irish, Native Americans, and Africans make-up the meats, the main contributors to the gumbo. The Italians, Dutch, and Portuguese make for nice spice to round out the ingredients. Gumbo must be eaten over rice, and for our cultural gumbo, the rice is America. For our survival, we must make certain some juice remains in the bowl. No one likes dry gumbo.

Hardy Jones is author of the novel *Every Bitter Thing* (Black Lawrence Press, 2010) and the memoir *People of the Good God* (Mongrel Empire Press, 2015). His fiction and creative nonfiction have been nominated for two Pushcart Prizes, and his creative nonfiction has been awarded two grants. His short stories were anthologized in the *2009 Dogzplot Flash Fiction Anthology*, *The Best of Clapboard House Literary Journal*, *Southern Gothic: New Tales of the South*, and *Summer Shorts II*. He is the co-founder and Executive Editor of the online journal *Cybersoleil* (cybersoleiljournal.com), and he is the Flash Fiction Editor for *Sugar Mule* (sugarmule.com). Dr. Jones teaches writing and serves as Director of Creative Writing at Cameron University. He splits his time between Lawton, Oklahoma and Si Sa Ket Province Thailand.

Website: www.hardyjoneswriting.com
Twitter: @HardyJonesWrite

Praise for *People of the Good God*

With an insider's ear for dialect and an outsider's eye for detail, Hardy Jones draws a compelling portrait of his people, the Cajuns of southwestern Louisiana. I found myself surprised and delighted by this friendly and informative journey through Cajun country. Jones proves a most amiable guide to the language, food, music, and complex character of this often misunderstood culture.

—Rilla Askew, author of *Kind of Kin*

In exacting and lucid prose combined with an extraordinary gift in capturing dialogue, Hardy Jones tells the story of how he not only learned to penetrate the heart of his Cajun cultural heritage but came to passionately embrace its indispensable significance to his core identity as a human being. Through a detailed and fascinatingly informative exploration of Cajun food, music, and language, he presents a proud, resilient culture and his integral place therein, fighting discrimination and intrusive encroachment from all sides for centuries, only to preserve its unique and exquisitely beautiful "way of life." In coming to terms with his own bloodline, Jones bestows his readers with the courage and insight to explore, accept, and appreciate their own.

—Larry D. Thomas
Member, Texas Institute of Letters
2008 Texas Poet Laureate

www.ingramcontent.com/pod-product-compliance
Lightning Source LLC
Chambersburg PA
CBHW070207100426
42743CB00013B/3083